Y0-DNM-037

PROCLAIM MY WORD

PROCLAIM MY WORD

Insights to Inspire Confidence in Members and Missionaries

by

S. Shane Littlefield

Timpanogos Publishing Company
Provo, Utah

© 1995 S. Shane Littlefield

All rights reserved. No part of this book may be reproduced in any form or by any means without permission in writing from the publisher, Timpanogos Publishing Company, P.O. Box 68, Provo, Utah, 84603.

ISBN 0-9647847-1-8

Library of Congress Catalog Card Number: 95-61399

PROCLAIM
MY WORD

Table of Contents

Prologue

Purpose

Proclaim My Word is written to convince you that **you** can do missionary work. Whether you are a prospective missionary, or a member who simply lacks confidence in your ability to share the gospel, it is designed to help you see that even you can be the cause of great miracles.

Content

It begins by helping you see that missionary work is part of a perfect plan. As your understanding and appreciation of the plan increases, so will your love for our Heavenly Father and our brothers and sisters throughout the world. You will see that a strong desire to share the gospel comes naturally, as a result of love.

This book also demonstrates that everyone really wants what you have. That is, they want to be happy. The restored gospel of Jesus Christ is the only key to real, lasting happiness. It points out that Satan will place obstacles in your way to keep you from learning these truths and sharing them with others. It also discusses specific principles that will enable you to overcome such obstacles.

But perhaps the greatest thing you will learn from this book is that no matter who you are, or what concerns you may have, even **you** can make a difference. No matter how inadequate you may feel, no matter how uneducated you may be, or even how limited your understanding and testimony of the gospel may be at the present time, you can--with the Lord's help--be the instrument in bringing to pass great and marvelous things. You can literally be the instrument the Lord uses to move mountains.

Approach

This book contains true stories to illustrate and emphasize the specific principles and doctrines taught. In each situation, typical missionaries and members experience great success in missionary work by obeying true principles.

This book is intended to be an aid to your study of these doctrines from the scriptures. Therefore, scriptural references are included prominently within the text. I strongly recommend that, as you read, you take time to read and ponder these scriptures.

Responsibility

As with any work of this type, I feel it important to claim sole responsibility for what is presented. Statements are not intended to represent official positions of the Church of Jesus Christ of Latter-day Saints or any of its departments or organizations.

I am also grateful to the leaders, friends and associates who have directly or indirectly contributed to the book's development. The greatest thanks goes to my beautiful wife and children for their patience and love. In addition, it would be inappropriate not to acknowledge the righteous example of the many missionaries who are serving the Lord throughout the world at any given time. They are truly one of the great miracles of our day. Observing and participating with them in this great work has made this book possible.

Chapter 1 - The Work:
The Great Plan of Happiness

I. VISION

We must see missionary work as a critical and beautiful part of the Great Plan of Happiness.

Sharing Happiness

Not long ago, I helped one of my daughters learn to ride her bicycle without the training wheels. I would get the chance to do so only once in her lifetime, so I savored every moment. I tried to be firm, but loving. I wanted it to be something she would remember. As she peddled around the neighborhood, one of our neighbors commented that she could not tell who was more proud, my daughter or I. When my daughter, Mckelle, was sufficiently tired, I gave her a big hug and told her how proud I was of her. To which she responded, "Let's call Grandma and Grandpa!" We wasted no time in breaking the news.

This little experience could be considered a microcosm of the Great Plan of our Heavenly Father. As we experience the joys that come from learning about and being able to participate in this plan, our natural feeling is to want to share them with others. Nothing is more pleasing to our Heavenly Father. Sharing the gospel brings great joy to both the *sharer* and the *sharee*. This is the reason our Heavenly Father commands all of us to share what we have. Missionary work is a responsibility we all share. But more importantly, it is an opportunity we all share.

Fruits of Happiness

As a loving father, Alma, sought to teach truths to his struggling son Corianton that would humble him and make him an instrument in bringing "souls unto repentance" (Alma 42:31). In so doing, he used the titles "plan of mercy" and "plan of redemption" to illustrate our Father's intentions in giving us the great opportunities of a mortal experience (vs. 11, 15). Mercy and redemption are both major aspects of the plan. But as President Boyd K. Packer has pointed out, Alma uses another phrase that seems to convey the message best, "the Great Plan of Happiness" (vs. 8).[1]

Wickedness is not happiness (Alma 41:10). Righteousness is happiness--in the most complete sense of the word. As missionaries to the world, our intent is to bring souls to Christ so that they can experience "the joy of the saints" (Enos 1:3). The fruits of the gospel are indeed "desirable above all" (1 Nephi 8:12). And "Men are that they might have joy" (2 Nephi 2:25).

The Joy of Light

As father Lehi, Saints the world over who experience blessings from living the truths of the gospel naturally desire to share that light and joy with their immediate families as well as their brothers and sisters of all circumstances (1 Nephi 8:12). This is pleasing to our Father in Heaven because so many of His children are working their way through the darkness of mortality with only

---

[1] From an address entitled, *The Great Plan of Happiness*, delivered at the annual CES symposium, August 10, 1993, Brigham Young University, p.2.

flickers of light. When people are surrounded by "exceedingly great mist[s] of darkness" (1 Nephi 8:23), the light of Christ is often all they have to cling to as they grope for a rod of iron. No wonder we are commanded to "let [our] lights so shine" (Matt. 5:16, 3 Nephi 12:16).

There is great joy in heaven when the light of truth begins to burn in a bosom where primarily darkness existed before (Luke 15:7). There must surely be similar joy for the son or daughter of God who by sharing the gospel helps to cause the heart of another son or daughter to burn. For not only has real happiness entered into life of another eternal family member, but "how great" shall be the joy of the messenger (D&C 18:15-16)!

The Vision of Building the Kingdom

Whether you are preparing to serve as a full-time missionary, stake missionary or member missionary who simply wants to learn how to better share the gospel, understanding the role of missionary work in this great plan is critical. It is critical because it affects your perspective and vision.

There is an example commonly used in management training that illustrates the importance of perspective and vision in any assignment. It has to do with an automobile manufacturing plant. Supposedly, there were two men who worked in entry level positions at the plant. Their entire work day consisted of performing the same task over and over again. They were in charge of putting bolts into the bumpers of the cars. One day the CEO of the company was touring the plant and he asked the two men about their jobs. The first responded negatively saying, "It's not much of a job. All I do is sit here and put these bolts in these bumpers."

The second man, whose perspective and vision was much broader responded, "Well, it's true that we do the same thing over and over

3

again, but what we are really doing is making cars. We are making sure these bumpers are fastened well because bumpers are important parts of a car. If the people who buy these cars ever get into accidents, the bumpers may save their lives."

The second man had perspective and vision. He knew that the day- to-day tasks of bumper assembly did not always require the greatest degree of intellectual or even physical prowess. But he could also see clearly his role in the assembly of the vehicle. He knew that he served a small, usually unnoticed, yet very important function that contributed directly to the overall success of the company.

As members of the church, sometimes things seem to get out of focus. During such moments, it is hard to see the Lord's work in the proper perspective. Our vision becomes limited. Somehow, we become too caught up in the details of day-to-day life. We lose sight of the eternal, and focus on the temporal. We may, for example, lose sight of the spiritual aspect of service and focus too much on the details of how much effort it is going to take to carry it out. We may wonder if it is really going to make much difference if we do our home/visiting teaching, take the sacrament to the elderly person down the street or take the youth on one more activity.

If this happens, fulfilling our responsibilities as members of the Lord's church to do missionary work can seem quite burdensome. In fact, it may not seem very important. We may not even be able to imagine it being worth all the effort. It must please the adversary to see us feel this way.

I marvel at the vision and perspective of the early saints. How much vision would it have taken for that little group gathered in the home of Peter Whitmer, Sr. in Fayette, New York on April 6, 1830 when the church was first organized? At that time, there was no shortage of churches. Religious excitement was spreading wildly. Several faiths were becoming well-established. It could have been difficult, under such circumstances, to see the need to organize yet another church.

But they were filled with the Spirit of the Lord. True testimonies of Christ burned in their souls. They were able to discern truth from error. They could feel the lack of spiritual nourishment available to the world. They had tasted of the truth restored through the prophet Joseph. T

his gave them vision. This enabled them to begin to comprehend the significance of what they were doing that day. Countless examples of equal vision permeate the history of the restored church. I would like to share one recent example.

A young Branch president arrived at Sacrament meeting. It was in an area where the Church was not yet very strong. As he stood to conduct the meeting, there were only eleven people present. He said, "Brothers and Sisters, as I drove to church this morning I passed by several other churches, all of which seemed to be full to the brim. When I arrived here there were only eleven of us."

"At first I was discouraged. I thought to myself, `If this is the Lord's church, why are there only eleven of us?' But then the Spirit whispered to me, `They only have part of the truth,' and I realized that they would therefore, not experience opposition to the degree we do. As we sang the opening hymn, I looked out at each of you and thought to myself, `the adversary will do whatever he can to keep people from attending this church, *yet there are eleven of us here anyway!*'"

Seeing the big picture seems to be one of the important challenges of life. The Lord took Moses up on a mountain and showed him the "big" picture. His response was enlightening. "Now, for this cause I know that man is nothing, which thing I never had supposed" (Moses 1:10). Once he was able to see the potential of

5

a soul through the Great Plan of Happiness, all of the strength and wisdom of mortal, worldly man became as "nothing."

Missionary work is much the same. Once we catch the vision of the far reaching effects that even a little effort can have, that effort suddenly becomes more important. The first step in preparing for missionary service is, therefore, to understand the absolutely awesome opportunity that is before us, and at least begin to comprehend the effects of bringing a soul to Christ (Moroni 8:16). As we do so, fear flees from our minds and hearts, and our divine nature as sons and daughters of God emerges. We no longer see through the glass as, "darkly" (1 Corin. 13:12). The purpose of life becomes more clear. The commandment to share becomes more meaningful. The words of living prophets become more valuable to us.

II. BELIEVING

In addition to seeing missionary work in the proper perspective, we also need to believe that the Lord can use each of us to accomplish great things.

Chocolate Milk

Life can be scary for a six-year-old. There I was, a first-grader, at school lunch. At my school it was "cool" to buy an extra chocolate milk with your lunch. The big guys bought and drank two. I had thought about buying an extra, but could never quite finish one, so I never indulged. But this day was unusual.

I was particularly pensive and excited this day because something wonderful had just happened in my family. A baby sister had just been born. Up to that point it had just been my brother and me. My parents had previously joked about what an ordeal it was going to be to have Dad fix dinner for a couple of days while

PROCLAIM MY WORD

Mom was still in the hospital. So as I was standing in the lunch line--extra change in my pocket--I got a brilliant idea. I would buy three extra chocolate milks! This would help Dad with his dinner assignment. As I paid for my lunch, I proudly announced that I would be purchasing four cartons of chocolate milk!

After lunch, I returned my tray to the appropriate counter. To my horror, and before I could do anything about it, the woman behind the counter snatched away my three extra cartons! She then proceeded to scold me for buying more than I could drink! I was so upset. I ran from the cafeteria sobbing. When my teacher discovered my dilemma she took me to the principal's office, and he marched me back down to the cafeteria. Together we confronted whom I considered to be the "evil" lunch lady. Once the principal helped her see my intentions, she apologized and promptly returned my three cartons of chocolate milk.

Learn and Believe

I learned a lot that day. I learned that it is important to know where you stand. I thought I was doing a good thing. It never occurred to me that someone might question my intentions. When they did, I shrank, because I did not know enough to stand up for what I was trying to do. My knowledge was limited, and so was my conviction. I thought I knew that what I was doing was right. But for a moment, she caused me to wonder. I saw the whole situation as an obstacle too overwhelming to handle. So I ran.

A similar thing often happens with regard to missionary work. We may feel impressed to do more, to begin fulfilling our responsibility to share the gospel, but presently we meet with obstacles. Too often, we back down or run away because we do not know enough about the whole situation to believe that we can overcome those obstacles. As we learn more about missionary work and how each of us can participate successfully, we become more confident in our ability to do it. We begin to believe that

7

we can do it. No matter who we are, or how many weaknesses we may have, we begin to see the whole concept of missionary work differently.

Believing We Are "Worthy of Hire"

If we are to be successful in our missionary efforts, an important part of our vision must be to understand and believe that "the laborer *is* worthy of his hire" (D&C 31:5 - *italics added*). Or, in other words, that the Lord does not call people (hire them), to participate in His work unless they are capable (worthy), of experiencing success in that assignment.

Does this sound familiar? It is simply another way of stating that powerful and timeless response of faithful Nephi to the inspired direction of his father, "I will go and do the things which the Lord hath commanded, for I know that the Lord giveth no commandment unto the children of men save he shall prepare a way for them to accomplish the thing which he commandeth them to do" (1 Nephi 3:7). President Thomas S. Monson has long taught this same truth with the beautiful adage, "Whom the Lord calls, the Lord qualifies."[2] He also shares the wise counsel, "When you are on the Lord's errand, you are entitled to the Lord's help."[3]

It is true that each of us has weaknesses and is subject to temptation. This is an important part of the plan. One of Satan's most successful strategies, however, is to encourage these feelings of inadequacy. He loves to entice the righteous to feel the wrong kind of sorrow for their sins and weaknesses (2 Corin 7:9-10,

---

[2]   From an address given at the Seminar for New Mission Presidents - Missionary Training Center, Provo, Utah - June 21, 1994. Used by permission.

[3]   Ibid.

PROCLAIM MY WORD

Mormon 2:12-14). Such feelings are offensive to the spirit of God. Without the spirit, it is impossible to see life and missionary work in the proper perspective.

In moments such as these, we forget our divine heritage and somehow begin to believe that we are just fallen, mortal creatures. It is not unlike the beautiful young person who looks in the mirror and sees the one tiny blemish on his or her face as though it were so prominent as to overpower all of the other attractive features. It is hard to let our lights so shine in such circumstances.

One of the lines the adversary and his followers often whisper is, "You can't be a missionary, you are not perfect. You make too many mistakes." He will play on any weakness he can. Perhaps we are not perfect in our relationships with others. Perhaps we are not doing well financially. The list goes on and on.

Another big one is, "You do not know the gospel well enough. What if someone asks a question and you don't know the answer?" He also loves to get us to compare ourselves with others. He may say, "Leave preaching the gospel to those who know it better than you."

When we allow Satan to tempt us into believing such lies, he wins. If he can keep us from even attempting to share the gospel, our chances for success are virtually zero. He knows that an ounce of prevention is worth a pound of cure. He does whatever he can to discourage us before we even begin. But as we begin to serve in faith, each of us will come to know that the Lord can make us "worthy of hire."

Every Member

He, therefore, commands each of us to share the Great Plan of Happiness with everyone. At His ascension, He gave the charge: "Go ye therefore, and teach all nations, baptizing them in the

9

name of the Father, and of the Son, and of the Holy Ghost: Teaching them to observe all things whatsoever I have commanded you..." (Matthew 28:19-20). This charge was not given solely to those who were with Him at the time, but was meant for all of us. "Every member a missionary," was the phrase so often used by President David O. McKay.[4]

Prospective missionaries, as well as all members of the church, who want to better fulfill their stewardships will develop faith in the Lord and in their own individual ability to be effective tools in the Lord's hands as they better understand their unique and glorious role in sharing the Great Plan of Happiness. This vision will produce, as a natural result, greater love for our Heavenly Father and His children, and the desire to share His word. As the Lord counseled Hyrum Smith, "Seek not to declare my word, but first seek to obtain my word, and then shall your tongue be loosed; then, if you desire, you shall have my Spirit and my word, yea, the power of God unto the convincing of men" (D&C 11:21).

---

[4] Conference Report, October 1965. © The Church of Jesus Christ of Latter-day Saints. Used by permission.

Chapter 2 - The Charge: Into All the World

I. THE LOVE OF AN ETERNAL FATHER

Our Heavenly Father commands us to share the gospel because He loves all of His children.

Parenthood

As a father, I have often been amazed at how much I love my children. There are times when I wonder if there is anything I would not do for them. Recently, for example, my three-year-old son, Joshua, approached me with all the love of heaven in his eyes and said, "Dad, I was just wondering how much I love you."

The other evening, my daughter Mckelle and I were watching a video together, popcorn in hand. No one else was home. We laughed and joked. But after a moment she got serious. She looked up at me with her big brown eyes and said, "Dad? You'll always be my Daddy; right?"

It is absolutely impossible to express the depth of love that I have for my children. Having experienced this kind of love for someone gives me a taste of, but also makes it all the more difficult for me to comprehend, how much our Heavenly Father loves us--His children.

11

He Is Our Father

What do we mean when we say that God is our Father? How do we feel about Him? Most people believe in God. There is too much evidence to suggest otherwise (Alma 30:40,44). We know that He is the father of our spirits. But what kind of relationship do we have with Him?

Many, within and without the church, have already developed a close, personal relationship with Him. Often this relationship has been developed without, or even in spite of, formal instruction or teaching. It is a spiritual relationship (John 4:23). He is the Father of our spirits (Romans 8:16). As our missionaries teach investigators about our Heavenly Father, they find it is common for them to already know a great deal about His nature and attributes.

Investigators often describe our Heavenly Father accurately. Occasionally, they are even surprised to hear themselves do so. They did not know they knew Him so well. Even when conflicts emerge between the truth they are learning and the creeds, teachings or official doctrines of other religions with which they may have associated, I have yet to hear someone retract his or her description of our Father in Heaven. I am confident this is because the spirit of the Lord whispers truth to the souls of honest, sincere truth-seekers everywhere (Alma 16:16).

They know what is right because they feel that it is right. They already know the plan. You may have heard the saying, "Every one is Mormon, they just forgot it when they were born." It is true that the great plan was presented to us, in its entirety, in the great council in heaven. Every person, no matter how they may act now or what they may do, shouted for joy at the opportunity to participate in this plan. Each and every one of us chose to follow the Savior and participate in this mortal experience (Job 38:7, Abraham 3).

In fact, most returned missionaries will tell you that it is quite common to hear new investigators say something like this, "We know that what you are teaching us is true, in fact, it all sounds quite familiar--like we have heard it all somewhere before." Our Father is merciful in teaching His children through the Spirit (D&C 4:7).

Missionaries find great treasures as they draw upon the incredible amount of spiritual instruction that each person with whom they work (member or non-member) has already received from the Lord. He, through the Holy Ghost, is the only perfect tutor (John 14:26).

Not long ago, I had the blessing of participating in the baptism of a dear friend. She met her future husband, a close friend (and now our dentist as well), while she was in law school. As she began seriously investigating the church, she wondered how anyone could consider one church to be the *only* true church. She grew up faithfully attending another church. The confusion was because of the fact that she already loved her Heavenly Father. And she knew He loved her.

She had developed a close relationship with Him. As a result, she was kind to His children. She lived as righteously as she could. She knew that her Father in Heaven had blessed her often. From the experiences she shared, it was obvious that He had blessed her in many situations throughout her life.

It is likely that her former church contributed somewhat to her desire to please God. But as she spoke, it became obvious that the degree of love that she had for her Father in Heaven could only have come through the intimations of the Spirit, and experiences in which she had exercised her faith in God and been blessed. She now has access to the fullness of the gospel. Many throughout the history of the world have had similar experiences.

13

THE CHARGE: INTO ALL THE WORLD

A Perfect Plan for His Children

Though we were placed on this earth with a veil of forgetfulness over our minds, our Father loves us too much to leave us here alone, without any guidance. Some of us have had the blessing of coming in direct contact with the entire reservoir of spiritual knowledge available to mortal man. Many others will not have that blessing (Matthew 7:14). But just as a parent would never refuse to feed a hungry child (Matt. 7:9-11), our Father in Heaven has established provisions in the Great Plan that allow all of us access to truth. The light of Christ and power or influence of the Holy Ghost are two such gifts.

These gifts have allowed countless of our brothers and sisters to follow truth, at least to some degree, without a knowledge of the fullness of the gospel. Were it not so, there could be no agency, probation or preparation for many here in mortality. Their only purpose in mortality would be to gain a physical body. The plan would have been frustrated. Just as opposition is necessary (2 Nephi 2:11), there must also be a law (Alma 42:17-22), ways to learn truth from God (John 14:26, Romans 10:13-14, D&C 50:17-22), and a way to judge between real and purported truth (Moroni 7:12-14, D&C 50:23-24).

II. AN URGENCY OF LOVE

As we understand the great need for the gospel in people's lives, we will feel an urgency to share it with others. That urgency will be motivated by love.

Who Is Responsible For Helping Whom?

Though this life is often referred to as a vale of tears, near-Celestial moments can cause many of those tears to be tears of joy. Contrasting such moments with the dark consequences of sin

14

in which so many of our brothers and sisters grope for light, will give us a feeling for the urgency with which our Father commands us to proclaim His word "Go ye into all the world and preach the gospel to every creature" (Mark 16:15). He must be greatly pained to see such suffering in ignorance. Jeremiah recorded these inspiring words of the Lord: "Behold, I will send for many [missionaries]...for mine eyes are upon all their ways; they are not hid from my face, neither is their iniquity hid from mine eyes" (Jeremiah 16:16-17).

When the Church of Jesus Christ of Latter-day Saints was still in its infancy, the Lord said, "And again, I say unto you, I give unto you a commandment, that every man, both elder, priest, teacher, and also member, go to..., labor..., to prepare and accomplish the things which I have commanded....every man to his neighbor..." (D&C 38:40-41).

He also said, "And thou shalt declare glad tidings, yea, publish it upon the mountains, and upon every high place, and among every people that thou shalt be permitted to see...to all; yea, preach, exhort, declare the truth" (D&C 19:29,37).   Others were commanded to, "proclaim my gospel from land to land, and from city to city, yea, in those regions round about where it has not been proclaimed" (D&C 66:5). Many times He has declared that the gospel will be preached to "every nation, kindred, tongue and people" (Mosiah 15:28). It is clear that our Father is desirous that many more of His children hear and receive the message of the restoration. He declared that His work and glory is "to bring to pass the immortality and eternal life" of man (Moses 1:39).

Therefore, He lays down strict commands to those who have the truth. Modern prophets have made it clear that every member of the church has a responsibility to do missionary work. It is not optional. Nor is it a responsibility that we can take casually. Its effects are far-reaching. There is responsibility associated with truth, light and knowledge "For of him unto whom much is given, much is required" (D&C 82:3). Perhaps this is because of the far-reaching effects of sharing the gospel. Let me tell you about a family whose experiences illustrate such effects.

Mighty Changes

When missionaries first knocked on their door, the woman of the home silently motioned for them to come back later because her husband was drunk. They asked her when they should return. This time they found the father sober. He was anxious to change his life, and allowed them to begin teaching him and his family the gospel. As they got to know each other, the missionaries learned that the mother worked outside the home and was financially supporting the family. The father's time was spent drinking alcohol and recovering from its effects. Most of the family's resources were wasted therein.

During that first visit, the spirit of the Lord touched their hearts and the light of truth began to flicker in their lives. They progressed rapidly. In what can only be described as a miraculous and immediate way, this man totally abandoned the vice that had plagued him and his family for literally generations. The couple and a daughter progressed rapidly after discovering their true nature as sons and daughters of God and being taught how to communicate more fully with Him. A few weeks later, they were baptized and confirmed members of the church. It was a glorious experience. Think of the difference the truths of the gospel make in their lives.

But as wonderful as it was, what happened to their son seemed even more touching. We will call him "Johnny." He was just eleven years old at the time. The Elders first met him during one of the discussions they were having with his parents and sister. In the middle of a spiritual discussion, he burst into the room, tracking mud on his feet and began to spew obscenities. He picked up a book, threw it against the wall and left. The

16

missionaries were a little confused. They were not sure whether he was member of the family, or a pint-sized terrorist.

Their opinion of him drifted toward the latter as the days went by. They learned from his parents that Johnny was part of a gang of young boys that spent most of their time causing mischief. The missionaries were the lucky beneficiaries of some of that mischief. Vandalizing the car they drove, throwing rocks at them as they passed, and regularly and purposefully disrupting their discussions with his family were just a few of his antics. The group he spent time with was also using drugs and alcohol. His parents were concerned, but did not know what to do.

Once they became members of the church, their desire to help Johnny increased. A few weeks after they were baptized they approached the Elders and asked if they could bring their son to church with them on Sunday. The missionaries had suggested it earlier, but the parents were not willing to try. Of course, the Elders responded enthusiastically.

No one will ever forget that Sunday. They thought it might be a little difficult for the particular primary teacher upon whose class he would be descending, so they forewarned the Primary president. After primary, the Primary president cornered the missionaries and said, "Don't you **ever** bring that child here again!" Well, they brought him back anyway, and after a couple of weeks he had made friends with some boys in his class. As the weeks went by, he spent less and less time with his gang, and more and more time with his new friends who were members of the church. He began to change. His desire to choose the right grew. He was eventually baptized and confirmed a member of the church.

When one of the Elders finished his mission, the entire family came to the airport to see him off. As Johnny entered the terminal he came running up, threw his arms around him and gave

17

him a big hug. The Elder hardly recognized Johnny because he had changed so much.   As they talked, Johnny shared an experience that typified the change that had occurred in his life. It went something like this:

"Guess what, Elder? Today, at school, I got my lunch and sat down to eat. Before I ate, I bowed my head and prayed. When I looked up, the guys across the table were laughing at me. But you know what? *I didn't even care, because I know you're supposed to pray when you eat*!"

This experience illustrates the kinds of changes that come into people's lives through the gospel. This young man had changed. In a few short months, he was a different person. Because of the restored gospel of Jesus Christ, he had changed from a "terror" to a wonderful young man. His life was dramatically different, and his future will in all likelihood be dramatically different. He now has access to all the truth he will ever need to reach his ultimate potential.

Think of the difference the gospel has made in his life. Ponder, if you will, the kind of mortal experience he would likely have had without the truth. Then ponder the kinds of things he will now be likely to experience if he remains faithful. Imagine how this must make his Father in Heaven feel.

Great joy also came into the hearts of the missionaries as they were allowed to participate with the Lord in bringing to pass a great miracle. These are the fruits of the Great Plan of Happiness. It is no wonder a loving Heavenly Father commands us to share what we have.

How Much Do We Care?

President VerNon A. Bingham was an example to me of this same degree of urgency motivated by love. I remember one day in particular in which, as a young missionary myself, he taught me a powerful lesson. It was preparation day. Those of us who were assigned to the office at the time got up and cleaned the entire office first thing in the morning. We cleaned the kitchen, polished the floors and straightened up the storage room. We then retreated to our desks to write our letters home. It was a stormy day. The rain came down in sheets. The dirt roads became quite muddy.

About midday, there was a knock at the door. It was the driver of a delivery truck. He announced that he had several cases of books to deliver. Almost before I could say anything, five or six men jumped out of the back of the truck and began carrying the books into the office. They were sweating, and covered with mud. The storage room was in the back, so they had to carry the books across our newly polished floor in order to put them away. Mud was everywhere. When they finished, I signed the receipt, and in an almost disgusted manner, I sent them on their way. I was not excited about starting the cleaning process all over again.

At that point the Mission President opened his office door. I watched him survey the scene. He looked at them. Then he looked at me. There was a look of worry on his face. Then he looked at them again, and again at me. The look on his face had increased to one of panic. The third time he looked at me, the look on his face could only be described as one of sheer horror. I thought to myself, "What!? It's just mud. We'll clean the floor...." But before I could say anything, he darted from his office, past the departing delivery men and shut the door so that everyone was inside. He stood in front of the door and said, "Nobody leaves this office without having heard the first discussion!" They accepted his invitation.

For the next ninety minutes, he proceeded to teach them the gospel. My companions and I were so embarrassed we just sat there quietly. When they left, each man had a copy of the Book of Mormon and a stack of pamphlets in his hands and the

President had a pocketful of names and addresses. Each man had accepted an invitation to receive the missionaries and be taught the gospel with his family.

Once they were gone, we all slithered back to our desks. As I sat there, I knew the phone was going to ring. I knew it was going to be the Mission President. After what seemed like an eternity, it rang. The voice on the line said, "Elder Littlefield, could you come in here for a minute." I thought to myself, "Well, this is it, I'm in big trouble!"

As I entered his office, he was sitting behind his desk with his head down. I sat down in the chair in front of his desk. After what seemed like another eternity, he looked up. He had tears in his eyes. He looked at me, and said quietly, with deep sincerity, "I just couldn't let them go. They would have walked out of here and never had another opportunity to hear the truth. I just couldn't let them go."

At that point I think I would have preferred a beating. We loved our Mission President. We would almost rather do anything than disappoint him. To this day, many of us are still in touch with him regularly. But I learned an invaluable lesson that day about the worth of souls. I learned that, to the greatest extent possible, the worth of each individual soul needs to be as great in our sight as it is in the sight of our Father in Heaven.

Even the Very Thought

Having caught the vision of the difference the gospel makes in peoples lives, "even the very thought" that some of their brothers and sisters would live and die without the truth caused the sons of Mosiah "to quake and tremble" (Mosiah 28:3). I have often wondered; "Do *I* quake and tremble to see my brothers and sisters in darkness?" I know I feel sorry for many people I see. It has been especially difficult as I have traveled. The more I see of different cultures and the world, the more I see the absolute desperate need for truth in which most people find themselves.

It has not always pained me to the point that I actually "quake and tremble," but I have shed tears at times. It hurts most to see the children. When the pure in heart and the innocent suffer the effects of the sins of others, it is sometimes more than I can bear. I think of my beautiful children. In such moments, I can understand why the Lord would say, "But whoso shall offend one of these little ones which believe in me, it were better for him that a millstone were hanged about his neck, and that he were drowned in the depth of the sea" (Matt. 18:6).

I grew up in happy circumstances. We were not rich, but we had enough. And we had plenty of love. My children will not likely be heirs to great temporal fortunes either, but they will know love. I am teaching them the truths of the restored gospel. As with most parents who have the gospel, to even entertain the thought that any one of my own children might ever be abused, neglected, or wanting of love or truth, does literally cause me to quake.

Imagine how difficult it must be at times, for our Father to see so many of His children in difficult circumstances. Literally millions of our brothers and sisters suffer untold consequences of sin and transgression everyday. So much could be avoided if they only knew better. It is ironic that many do not even know what is happening to them. Some even insist that they have all the happiness they need.

The fact that our Heavenly Father would send His children to earth to pass through such experiences gives us insight into how much He values the principle of agency upon which the plan is based. Our blessing, as missionaries, is the opportunity to help others exercise that agency and avoid such consequences.

THE CHARGE: INTO ALL THE WORLD

Chapter 3 - The Message: Restored Truth

I. EVERY GOOD THING

The Spirit testifies of all truth. Truth can be found in many different places. People want truth. People need more truth. The gospel is restored, saving truth.

Virtuous, Lovely, Of Good Report

As members of the church, we seek after all truth. Through John, the Lord taught that the "Spirit of truth" would guide us "into all truth" (16:13). Truth is everywhere. Indeed there is beauty all around. The thirteenth Article of Faith declares that we seek after anything "virtuous, lovely, of good report or praiseworthy." This is because all truth glorifies God. Alma said, "all things denote there is a God" (30:44). Let me share with you some examples of beauty and truth of which the Spirit has testified to me, but which may not always be thought of as spiritual.

Christmas

The first and most obvious is the Christmas season. Each year, people all over the world take time from their busy lives to contemplate the life the our Savior. Goodwill abounds. There is a special feeling of love, often acknowledged by even the crustiest of skeptics. Random acts of kindness become more commonplace. It is a time of sharing, rejoicing, being grateful and expressing love.

PROCLAIM MY WORD

Of course many do not believe in Jesus Christ. And, even among those who profess to, there are many different degrees of understanding and appreciation for Him, His life and His Atonement.

Yet at Christmastime, there always seems to be sufficient kindness, compassion and righteousness to invite a special witness from God that the birth and life of His Only Begotten were transcendent events worth celebrating. Everyone seems to feel the Spirit during the Christmas season.

A Dance of Dedication

In September of 1994, Heather Whitestone, Miss Alabama became the first physically challenged Miss America. It was an inspiring event. Against what many would consider overwhelming odds she won the title, taking first place in the major portions of the competition. But what won the hearts of millions watching, and apparently the judges as well, was the ballet dance she performed during the talent portion of the competition.

It would have been impressive had it been performed with equal grace by any young woman. But this performance was special. The casual observer may never have known that due to a childhood illness, Miss Whitestone was deaf. She was not able to hear the music to which she danced. She danced by memorizing the written music, counting the beats, and trying to feel the message of the lyrics. She danced to music about the life and atonement of the Savior.

A sweet spirit bore witness to me that the beautiful performance I was watching was the result of countless hours of unusual dedication and heartbreaking effort. The diverse audience was so moved that by the middle of the dance they were on their feet cheering. As she finished they remained on their feet.

Greater Love

A third example is one of great bravery and heroism. On January 13, 1982, Air Florida flight 90 from Washington, D.C. to Tampa, Florida crashed into the Potomac river just outside the nation's capital. Hundreds were cast into the icy waters. Rescuers struggled frantically to pull survivors from the river before they drowned. Through the miracle of modern media, the world watched as events unfolded. Few who witnessed the event will ever forget the heroism of a Mr. Arland D. Williams Jr.

While struggling for his life in the freezing water, a helicopter lowered a lifeline to him five times. Each time he bravely declined to be rescued himself, passing the line instead to another. When the line was lowered the sixth time he was gone. Even today, the thought that someone would do such a thing touches our hearts. "Greater love hath no man than this, that [he] lay down his life for his friends" (John 15:13). How do you feel as you read this true account? What could it possibly have in common with an unusual ballet dance and the Christmas season?

Truth

What these seemingly unrelated events have in common is truth. Each is a manifestation to one degree or another of something good. Moroni teaches that "all things which are good cometh of God" (7:12). He defines good as "every thing which inviteth and enticeth to do good, and to love God, and to serve him." He states that "every thing" that meets this criteria is "inspired of God" (vs. 13). The Spirit or Light of Christ testifies to us of such truth.

As people are exposed to more and more truth, the spirit--the power or influence of the Holy Ghost--will also come upon them, in corresponding degrees, to testify of such truth. This can, and regularly does, happen before a person has been baptized and received the gift of the Holy Ghost.[5] The promise of the Book of Mormon, that missionaries share with investigators throughout the world, is an example. Though they have not yet been baptized and received the gift of the Holy Ghost, they are still promised that "by the power of the Holy Ghost, [they] may know the truth of all things" (Moroni 10:5).

Attracted To Truth

People in general are attracted to truth, especially during unusually difficult or ponderous times. Many spend their lives in the pursuit of knowledge and wisdom through study (2 Tim. 3:7). Simply put, truth is inviting. There is something about it that resonates deep in our souls.

As we learn truth, we feel we are growing and maturing (D&C 50:22). We can sense its value. We can sense its goodness. Even the devils can recognize truth when they come in contact with it (Luke 4:33-35). There are several examples throughout this book that illustrate that many of our brothers and sisters throughout the world are interested in finding and learning more truth, for it brings them joy.

In Section 84 of *Doctrine and Covenants*, the Lord explains why truth resonates so profoundly within us and what happens if we hearken to it. He said, "Whatsoever is truth is light, and whatsoever is light is Spirit, even the Spirit of Jesus Christ. And the Spirit giveth light to every man that cometh into the world; and the Spirit enlighteneth every man through the world, that hearkeneth to the voice of the Spirit. And every one that hearkeneth to the voice of the Spirit cometh unto God, even the Father" (vs. 45-47).

---

[5]   See *Gospel Doctrine*, Joseph F. Smith, 1973, pp. 66-67.

THE MESSAGE: RESTORED TRUTH

As a teenager, I had the opportunity of working as a Page in the United States Senate in Washington, D.C. For me, it was a great experience. There were approximately thirty of us on the Senate side and seventy-five who worked on the side of the House of Representatives. I met young people from all over the country. Many of them were children of influential government leaders and their friends.

I also had the opportunity of observing, up close and for an extended period of time, those leaders who actually ran my country. I saw them in all kinds of circumstances. Perhaps I am unusually curious, but I watched them carefully and evaluated their every move. I learned a lot. I learned that there are people with good intentions and people with bad intentions everywhere. I learned that we, as members of the church, do not have a corner on the market for righteousness.

But I also saw a sharp, dramatic contrast between mortality with the fullness of the gospel and mortality without it. As my young colleagues would pursue their individual quests for happiness, most of them would follow the ways of the world and often end up miserable. It was fascinating for me to see how they responded to my presence. I did not participate in their experimentation with alcohol etc. And I was amazed at the number of morning-after telephone calls I received wherein several expressed embarrassment for their actions.

To their credit, they were generally quite tolerant and accepting of me and my standards. But the thing that impressed me most was the degree to which they were personally interested in learning more truth themselves. On more than one occasion I was asked what motivated me to live the way I did. Some even asked if they could attend church with me. In a less than effective way, I attempted to meet their needs, but I could have done much better.

Life Is a Quest for Truth and Happiness

Very few people, if any, desire to be miserable. The problem is that they look for truth and happiness in all the wrong places. Many try to find it in sin. It seems almost as if many do not know the difference between real, lasting joy and fleeting pleasure or gratification. Fun, lust, excitement and passion are other cheap substitutes for real happiness.

I observed something else interesting among the actual Members of Congress. I noticed that these people, who were making laws and setting government policy, were not much different than the people in my ward back in Utah--at least as far as basic human characteristics were concerned. Some of them were very bright, others were hard workers. There was a diversity of gifts and talents.

The big contrast could be seen in how they appeared to understand the purpose of life. With the possible exception of a few outstanding individuals and some members of the church, the moral authority most commonly cited as they argued their positions was limited in its reference to absolute truth.

Values that I often observed were comfort, convenience, speed, efficiency, power, influence and fame. Now, of course there were degrees of each. And I do believe most of these leaders were motivated by good intentions. They just seemed, from my limited, inexperienced point of view, to lack eternal perspective. Right and wrong often seemed relative.

The influences exerted upon them to represent individual interests over the good of the whole were tremendous. It seemed to me, that convictions were sacrificed to convenience regularly. It also seemed that they lacked a sense of mission, a sense of vision. That clear understanding of the purpose of life--that was so familiar in the members back home--seemed wanting. All of this in spite of the fact that these were all people of means, fame and influence whose mail was always addressed to the "Honorable" so and so.

I have had occasion since to observe--equally as close and for an extended period of time--General Authorities of the church. These are men whose every desire is to serve God, to publish peace and to serve humankind. These are men who, in spite of the high-profile nature of their positions, perform sweet acts of service while attempting to avoid recognition. I have been the beneficiary of such love and service. There is no lack of truth in their understanding of the purpose of life. With all of the responsibilities they bear and all of the pressures exerted upon them, there is never any compromise of principle in order to patronize.

In addition, these men always seem to be positive. When you enter the Church Administration Building there is a very sacred feeling. There is a tremendous sense of vision and an unequalled sense of mission. It is a feeling of hope, of excitement, of joy and of truth. There is no lack of moral authority in anything they say or do.

Degrees of Truth

To contrast these two groups of people produces a humbling vision. It is a vision of millions of our brothers and sisters throughout the world including government, education and civic leaders, moving their way through life with only a limited amount of light to guide their way. So many do so much with so little. And, as has often been said, many of us do so little with so much.

These are all our brothers and sisters. Our Father in Heaven has commanded us to help them taste of the sweet fruits of the restored gospel of Jesus Christ so that the atonement of His Only Begotten can bear full sway in their lives. Once they taste of such fruits, there will still be much work to do to help them continue to progress. Let us not give up before we have even begun. Let us not limit the scope of possibilities because of temptation. Many would-be missionaries have become discouraged when initial attempts to share the gospel with friends and relatives have met with resistance.

Satan knows that if he can frustrate our initial efforts, the likelihood of our trying again is greatly diminished. Therefore, let us exercise faith in the Lord and His ability to reach our brothers and sisters. Let us remember the power of the word (Alma 31:5). Let us raise our expectations as far as what can be accomplished-- the miracles that can be wrought. Everyone wants the happiness that comes from living truth.

Restored Truth

The truths we share with the world have come to us through living prophets in the latter days. Many of these truths existed on the earth previously, but were lost for a period of time. Because our Heavenly Father loves us, they have now been restored. We are the beneficiaries of this precious and sacred knowledge.

When the truth with which we come in contact is saving--pure and absolute--it resonates in a more profound, eternal way. The familiarity with which the saving truth of the restored gospel rings true is so convincing that it often causes people to dramatically alter their life's pursuits. People will leave their worldly nets and become "fishers of men" (Matthew 4:19). In *Doctrine and Covenants* Section 84, the Lord declares that "the word of the Lord is truth" (vs. 45). We know that the message which we share with the world is true. We know this because of the Spirit.

In *Doctrine and Covenants* Section 11, we learn that it is the Spirit that provides missionaries with "the power of God unto the convincing of men" (vs. 21). A person is convinced, or converted, spiritually as the Spirit testifies to his or her soul of gospel truths and he or she begins to live them. It is the Spirit that causes conversion.

Conversion is glorious. It brings great joy to all involved. This is because "man is spirit...and spirit and element, inseparably connected, receive a fullness of joy" (D&C 93:33). Spirit, intelligence, light and truth reject evil and thus resonate positively with the very elements of the soul of man (93:29-40, 88:15). When teaching by the Spirit has taken place "he that preacheth and he that receiveth...rejoice together" (50: 22). It was Father Lehi who, when he had tasted of the fruit, said that it was "most sweet" (1 Nephi 8:11).

II. THE GOSPEL OF JESUS CHRIST

The truths of the restored gospel of Jesus Christ are the answer to everything.

The Message of the Restoration

The fullness of truth found in the restored gospel of Jesus Christ is the formula for happiness and joy in this life and throughout the eternities (D&C 1, 14:7, 2 Nephi 2:25). We proclaim to the world that we know that there is a God in heaven. The message of the restoration is that Jesus Christ lives today, that He came to earth in the meridian of time, redeemed us all from the fall and atoned for the sins of all mankind. It is also that we can, through faith, repentance, baptism, receiving the gift of the Holy Ghost and enduring to the end, return again to Him (D&C 1).

It is that we are children of God, with the potential to become even as He is (Romans 8:16-17, Matthew 5:48, D&C 132:20). It is that He has given us these truths through living prophets of God

31

who have brought to light additional scripture, both ancient and modern. Chief among this scripture is the Book of Mormon which He has given us as the primary tool to convert the world. It is also that He speaks to man through these prophets. Finally, it is that He has established, once again, His Church to guide us in our journey through mortality.

What a glorious message! Can you think of any problem, any question, any ill that cannot find its solution in this message? Every plague, every evil, every sorrow, every vice is provided for. There is no wound that cannot find balm. There is no doubt that cannot be resolved. There is no loneliness that cannot find loving company.

"Jim" and "Julie" are examples of the difference these truths can make in peoples' everyday lives. They had experienced many of the difficulties that come as results of sin or transgression. There were problems with their marriage. Their beautiful young daughter was developing bad habits. Their financial situation was bad and getting worse. Jim's mother was bitter against the church. Julie had a rough time as a teenager. And the list went on.

It seemed as though they had tried to improve their situation, but felt the whole effort was futile. They were good people, with righteous desires. Yet their attitude was often pessimistic. Julie, especially, seemed discouraged with life.

It was miraculous to see what happened as member-missionaries descended upon them in love. It was not a single, great event that changed their lives. It was the truths of the restored gospel and the consistent efforts and examples of several people over a period of time. It began with a lot of listening. The members of the church around them tried to be good examples. Service was rendered, and righteous examples led to questions.

THE MESSAGE: RESTORED TRUTH

In appropriate settings and at appropriate times, testimony was shared and the Spirit was felt. After some time they expressed an interest in learning more. As they were taught, the Spirit was felt again and they were helped to recognize those feelings as coming from our Father in Heaven. They progressed slowly. But with time, they began to attend church.

As the spirit of the gospel began to enter their lives, member-missionaries helped them live the truths of the message of the restoration by inviting them to do so, and helping them keep those commitments. Local Priesthood leaders became involved. One, in particular, was a financial planner by profession. He sat down with Jim and Julie and helped them plan for their future. He also followed-up with them regularly. All of this effort helped tremendously, yet their progress remained painfully slow.

I wish I could report that everything was miraculously changed overnight, but it was not. It is now years later, however, and the consistent efforts of these many member-missionaries has begun to pay-off. Jim and Julie are preparing to enter the temple to be sealed together as a family for time and all eternity. They will be the first to say that they still have lots of work to do. But it is amazing to see the progress they have made.

As they progressed in their understanding of the truths of fullness of the restored gospel and began to apply them, their lives changed dramatically. Their perspective and vision became eternal, and hope became much more common than despair. Virtually every aspect of their lives has improved significantly. The atonement of the Lord has begun to take effect in their lives. These are the effects of truth. These are the effects of the message of the restoration.

How Much Will the Truth Really Help?

Those of us who suppose to have the fullness of the gospel sometimes wonder, however, why *we* still suffer these kinds of things? Perhaps this accounts for much of the hesitancy to share the gospel we exhibit. If we have not experienced the kind of relief we say is available through the truths of the restoration, what reason have we to assume that others will?

Under such an assumption, it would not make much sense to spend our time sharing the gospel with others. It would be like trying to sell someone a product that we thought was broken. I can think of two answers to the above question.

Recognizing Spiritual Blessings

First of all, it has been my experience that most of us *have* experienced great relief and blessings through living the truths of the restored gospel. We simply have not been very good at recognizing them. This has long been a common problem. A good friend, who was recently converted, confided in me that it was difficult for him to pay tithing. In fact, it was a principle that he prayed a lot about as he was being taught. He said that each time he paid it, he could not help but wonder what he might have done with the money.

He had been greatly blessed, temporally, since he began to live this important law. He had a difficult time determining, however, whether these blessings were the result of his obedience to an eternal law or coincidence. He jokingly asked, "When I go to tithing settlement, is the Bishop going to give me a statement listing which blessings I have received because I paid tithing and how much each cost?" My answer to him was, "Yes, and it will also indicate which tragedies, problems and misfortunes you avoided."

It would be nice if someone could provide us with an itemized monthly description of our commandment-keeping and the resulting blessings. For me, this practically does happen each week as I partake of the sacrament. It would be nice if everything were obvious all of the time. The only problem would be that the plan would be frustrated. It would be impossible for us to exercise our agency and to progress as planned. Learning to recognize spiritual blessings is often difficult (D&C 6:15, 22-23). Sometimes the best way to recognize when we are being spiritually blessed is to have those blessings denied us for a time. The absence of spiritual help can be very obvious.

Ye Shall Have Tribulation

Second, it is inappropriate to assume that just because we have the gospel we are going to slide through life with no tribulation. The Savior taught, "In the world ye shall have tribulation: but be of good cheer; I have overcome the world" (John 16:33). We also know that "whom the Lord loves he chastens" (D&C 95:1).

In fact, the more we learn, the more we can expect to face (Helaman 15:3, D&C 95:1, 101:5, 105:6, 136:31). This is one of the fundamental parts of the plan. No matter how great our knowledge of, or experience with, the truths of the gospel we may expect difficulties and trials (D&C 97:6, 1:25-28). Just as more and more heat is required to further purge precious metals of impurities, we will never be without the opportunity to grow and progress through challenges.

Our Heavenly Father loves us too much to allow us to waste our time here in mortality. "For behold, this life is the time for men to prepare to meet God; yea, behold the day of this life is the day for men to perform their labors..." (Alma 34:32-35). As we learn to rely upon the Savior and draw upon His atoning sacrifice, we can overcome and avoid the effects of sin.

PROCLAIM MY WORD

The Solution

The gospel is the answer, and everyone wants answers. In a very real sense, you could say that everyone wants what we have. This sounds like a presumptuous statement. But when you think about what we have, it makes more sense. Whether we recognize it or not, the restored gospel is the answer to all of life's questions. The degree to which we may or may not have experienced this ourselves, is irrelevant. The restored gospel *is* the only key to real, lasting happiness, and everyone wants to be happy.

Truth exists. It is absolute and universally applicable. We need to help others find and obtain it so that they can receive this happiness. Our Heavenly Father loves His children. He does not want us to suffer in ignorance, experiencing the consequences of sin and transgression. He wants us to be happy. It is this knowledge, of which the world is in such desperate need. It is the living of these truths that will eventually usher-in the second coming.

President Howard W. Hunter said, "We are in the work of saving souls, of inviting people to come unto Christ, of bringing them into the waters of baptism so that they may continue to progress along the path that leads to eternal life. This world needs the gospel of Jesus Christ. The gospel provides the only way the world will ever know peace. As followers of Jesus Christ, we seek to enlarge the circle of love and understanding among the people of the earth."[6]

---

[6] *Ensign*, November 1994, p.88. © The Church of Jesus Christ of Latter-day Saints. Used by permission.

Chapter 4 - The Message: Finding Truth

I. OBSTACLES

Our first task in sharing the gospel is helping people find or come in contact with truth. There are many obstacles to finding truth.

They Know Not Where to Find It

In a revelation regarding some of the persecutors of the church, the Lord explained that there are many "who are only kept from the truth because they know not where to find it" (D&C 123:12). As members of the church, we too often succumb to the adversary's efforts to convince us that what we have may be suitable for us, but most people would not be interested.

He is very cunning. He wants us to believe that thinking people, in particular, will not find the truths of the restored gospel logical or practical. He encourages the tendency which many of us have at times, to hide our candles under a bushel. He would have us be embarrassed because we are different from the world. He makes it easy to feel ashamed, to fall away and be lost (1 Nephi 8:19-28).

While it is true that we are a "peculiar people" (1 Peter 2:9), we are peculiar in the sense that we stand out as being special. Elder Russell M. Nelson explained, "In the Old testament the Hebrew term from which peculiar was translated is *cgullah* which means `valued property,' or `treasure.'"

"In the New Testament, the Greek term from which peculiar was translated is *peripoiesis*, which means `possession,' or `an obtaining.'

With that understanding, we can see that the scriptural term *peculiar*...signifies `valued treasure,' 'made' or `selected by God.' Thus, for us to be identified by servants of the Lord as his *peculiar* people is a compliment of the highest order."[7]

The scriptures tell us that the Lord has "put difference" between us and the world on purpose (Leviticus 10:10). It is so that the world can tell the difference "between holy and unholy, and between unclean and clean." He further explains, "For I am the Lord your God; ye shall therefore sanctify yourselves, and ye shall be holy; for I am holy" (11:44).

It is erroneous to assume that the truths of the gospel, and the resulting lifestyle are undesirable to most people. False interpretations and heresay may paint them as such, but the reality is that the truth is only undesirable to the unrepentant and the hard of heart (1 Nephi 16:2). Moreover, the power of the spirit will lead even many of them to repent (Alma 30).

Many examples can be found to illustrate the fact that the world is hungry for spiritual truth. It is much more than just a desire for order or world peace. People have an innate desire to fulfill the purpose for which they are here in mortality, to participate more fully in the Great Plan of Happiness. Laws have been made, great wars have been fought and people have given their lives to secure rights to worship according to their conscience, to think and learn freely and to pursue truth according to the desires of their hearts.

---

[7] From an address given at the CES Fireside, January 8, 1995, BYU Marriott Center. Used by permission.

THE MESSAGE: FINDING TRUTH

The modern media is an example of both an obstacle to finding truth and an evidence of the search for truth. No one would question that it is often one of the adversary's greatest tools. The entire industry often appears to be driven by profit and pride. We are constantly barraged with everything that is the opposite of "virtuous, lovely, of good report or praiseworthy." Many lives are destroyed through this medium.

Though these images are prevalent in our society today, they are not a reflection of what is in the hearts of most of our brothers and sisters throughout the world. Rather, they are part of a typical move by Satan to misuse these various mediums to his advantage. Books, music and the different forms of drama are all mediums that have great potential for communicating truth and beauty. The devil loves to destroy that which is beautiful. Yet, even in the midst of all of the violence and ugliness, we see an obvious example of the search for truth and light.

Sensationalism would not be sensational if the values of the vast majority of society were not righteousness and truth. Many of those who publish books, produce movies and plays and write music still seek to portray, uncover or promote some form of truth because people want it. The problem is that their reservoirs of truth are often dry or dangerously polluted. If we do not fill them with clear streams of living water, the adversary will fill them with the tainted water of the world.

The fact that people seek truth is an evidence of their spiritual desire for it. This is what our brothers and sisters throughout the world really want. They want truth. They want substance. They want to progress spiritually and fulfill the purpose for which they are here on the earth. They want to be happy. And the gospel is the only key to real, lasting happiness in this life and in the eternities.

Missionary work is simply giving them an opportunity to taste that real happiness. It is taking their hand, placing it on the iron rod, and helping them hold fast until they have tasted of the fruit. People who taste of the fruit never find it distasteful.

Subtle Craftiness

Another category of obstacles is also found in D&C 123:12. The Lord says that "there are many yet on the earth...who are blinded by the subtle craftiness of men." There are examples of this subtle craftiness everywhere we look. Those who have knowingly, or unknowingly, become tools in the hands of the adversary have created a picture that appears very enticing to truth seekers.

One of the more subtle, yet crafty tactics of the devil is the "spoonful of sugar helps the medicine go down" tactic. To get us to swallow evil, the devil often attempts to sugar coat it. He regularly attempts to link it to something good or desirable. Good music often has bad lyrics. Movies with artistic merit often include brief scenes that pollute and remain in the mind for a long time. None of us would think of eating poisoned food just because it tastes good. Yet through this tactic, many rationalize the consumption of spiritual poison saying in effect, "it is worth it." The Lord warned that in matters of truth, if possible, "even the very elect would be deceived" (JS-M 1:22).

Often Satan entices us to pursue interests which in and of themselves may not be harmful, but taken to an extreme can cause us to neglect things that are more important. I have learned that as I keep my priorities straight, the Lord blesses me in all the areas of my life. As I put the Lord and my family first, my professional and other interests are also blessed. It is true that He can make much more out of my life than I can on my own. The Lord knows all of my needs (3 Nephi 13:32), but He would have me pursue them in wisdom and in order.

As a young missionary, I remember being so anxious to do the Lord's work that, from time to time, I would schedule appointments on preparation day. I was willing to sacrifice even my own preparation to do the work. It did not take me long to recognize that the negative effect of not using the day for what it was intended was greater than any positive results achieved. I began to realize that it was there for a purpose. The Lord was providing me with an opportunity to prepare to be successful during the coming week. Similarly, I have been amazed at how the General Authorities, who are so busy building the kingdom, find time to sharpen the saw. Keeping our priorities straight also helps us avoid temptation.

Two full-time missionaries experienced the subtlety with which the adversary works. They were assigned to an area where missionaries had not been for several months. Soon after they arrived they met a man who seemed eager to hear their message. They agreed to teach him. During the first visit they discovered that this man had been in contact with the missionaries before, but for some reason had not continued investigating the church. Normally, these people are good contacts because the Spirit has worked with them in the interim. So the missionaries began to teach him. They did not take time to discover, however, exactly why this man had not been baptized after previous contacts with the missionaries.

They spent many hours with this man. He had more and more questions and seemed to thrive on having the Elders in his home. The visits became more frequent and lasted for longer periods of time. They found time to do little else. They felt that the more time they spent with this man, the more questions and concerns he raised. He could not seem to find time to read and pray about the Book of Mormon, attend church or do any of the things the missionaries asked of him. Yet, he was extremely anxious to have the missionaries visit.

They soon began to wonder whether or not he was sincerely interested in learning more about the gospel. They decided to investigate and discovered that this man had a long history of problems. They learned that several previous sets of missionaries had also spent hours of the Lord's time giving him opportunities to repent, but to no avail. He enjoyed the company of the servants of the Lord, but was not willing to repent of his sins. Had these missionaries been able to discover what was happening sooner, they might have been able to prioritize and use the Lord's precious time in a more valuable way.

Where Do Obstacles Come From?

It has been said that there are only two things in life that are certain: death and taxes. Well, I would like to add another to the list: opposition to the work of God. This third certainty is important for us to be aware of as we attempt to do missionary work. It is important to know that virtually all of the obstacles we will run into as we attempt to share the truth are inspired of the devil. He is the perpetrator of all evil. In one sense or another, it all originates with him. Even the obstacles that we face in our own minds and hearts.

He hatches and nurtures every awful, ugly and debasing idea, concept or principle. The scriptures tell us that "the devil is an enemy unto God, and fighteth against him continually, and inviteth and enticeth to sin, and to do that which is evil continually" (Moroni 7:12). The devil "persuadeth no man to do good, no, not one; neither do his angels; neither do they who subject themselves unto him" (7:17). His motivations for doing this are simple, "he seeketh that all men might be miserable like unto himself" (2 Nephi 2:27). He has sought to thwart the great plan ever since he fell.

Any time we set out to do that which is good in the sight of God, we can expect to meet with resistance. He will oppose any effort to be righteous, teach truth, or to do good because these things are pleasing unto God. They further His work. They are the very reasons this great plan was put in place (Moses 1:39). We can expect additional opposition, therefore, when we begin to share the saving truths of the gospel with others. The adversary will oppose these attempts, in particular, because they pose an even greater threat to his kingdom.

Error's Gloomy Ways

Since he is the embodiment of all that is bad, Satan must also be lazy. Therefore, it would not be inappropriate to assume that he and his followers will likely take the path of least resistance whenever possible. Once a person has grabbed hold of the iron rod and begun along the path that leads to eternal life and exaltation, the adversary will have to work much harder to persuade him or her to leave the path and become lost. He will have to put forth more effort because the individual has been connected with the true source of lasting spiritual power.

His task then becomes more difficult because the person is likely to have the spirit more often, and the spirit is offensive to evil. If a person clings to the iron rod, makes it to the tree, is able to partake of the fruit, and tastes its sweetness, it will require even more effort on the part of Satan to dissuade this person. With each ounce of truth learned, each portion of the spirit of God attained, he must intensify his efforts.

The devil knows that an ounce of righteousness-prevention is worth a ton of righteousness-destruction later. This is why he focuses so much effort on those who are beginning to learn about the gospel and those who are beginning to learn how to share the gospel. Once a missionary has received a call to serve but has not yet been set apart, he or she becomes a primary target. Satan turns up the heat. The same thing is true for people who begin investigating the church. He would rather stop them early before they become more of a problem. In these and other situations, being aware of the fact that opposition will likely arise, and knowing how to combat that opposition will help.

A Case of Opposition

Missionaries often notice the adversary working on their investigators between visits. I know a missionary who felt prompted on one occasion to do a little prevention of his own.

The Elder and his companion had just been introduced to a beautiful new investigator family by another wonderful family they had just had the blessing of baptizing. The "Smiths" were a couple in their forties with one teenage son, one teenage daughter and an eleven-year-old daughter. As the Elders taught them the first discussion one Saturday afternoon, both families were in attendance. The spirit was abundantly present. Everyone felt uplifted and closer to our Father in Heaven. They were all anxious for the second discussion, scheduled two days later.

Before leaving, however, one Elder felt unusually impressed to say something like this to the new investigator family: "Brothers and Sisters, what we have taught you today is true. And because it is true Satan does not like it. In fact, it is entirely possible that between now and Monday when we come back, he will attempt to discourage you from continuing to listen to us. Things may happen that will cause you to wonder whether or not what we have taught you is true. You may be tempted not to read the things in the Book of Mormon that we have asked you to read. You may be tempted not to pray for the spirit.

"If any of these things happen to you, will you remember that we warned you beforehand? Will you remember that it is only because the adversary does not like the fact that you are making significant spiritual progress? Your progress is a threat to his kingdom. He does not want you to be happy. He wants you to be miserable. Will you take any temptations that come as evidences of the truthfulness of what we are teaching you? If it were not so, the devil would not care. He would not bother you."

The spirit was present as he spoke, and the Smith family accepted the unusual invitation. This Elder had seldom been prompted to say this kind of thing, but he felt impressed to say it this time, and to do so with all the conviction he could muster. So he obeyed.

When he and his companion returned, only forty-eight hours later, they discovered why. Before they even reached the house, the youngest daughter came running up exclaiming, "Elders, Elders, look what someone gave us!" She handed him a piece of paper which was entitled something like, "Twenty-one Awful Things About Joseph Smith." The missionaries glanced at them, and sure enough they were awful!

They proceeded to the home, prayed with the family, and then asked, "Where did you get this?" The mother spoke up and said, "Right after you left, on Saturday, someone shoved this under our door." "Did you read it?" they asked. She said, "Yes." "And what did you think?" they asked again. "Well, at first I was quite confused, because this did not sound at all like the Joseph Smith you told us about. It caused me to wonder. But then I remembered what you said. And I thought to myself, `this must be one of those things designed to keep us from listening to the Elders,' so I put it away and didn't look at it again." The missionary then said to her, "Do you believe any of the things on that paper?" And she said, "No." The rest of the family agreed, and they tore the paper into pieces and threw it away.

But before they began teaching, this Elder felt impressed to ask, "By the way, did anything else by chance happen to discourage you from listening to us?" This time the father responded, "Yes. Late that same night, in the middle of the night, someone approached our home and threw big rocks onto our roof [which would have been awfully loud since the homes in that area of that country all had corrugated tin roofs]. They yelled `Mormons!, Mormons!' It really scared us. We didn't know quite what was happening. But then we remembered what you said and thought, `this must just be another one of those things the Elders warned us about.'"

You would think that this story would end here. But before continuing, the Elders asked again, "Did anything else happen?" Again the responses was, "Yes. The minister who preaches at the church down the street came to visit us yesterday. He told us that you are `sons of the devil,' and that if we keep listening to you we will go to hell." "Anything else?" "Yes! An old woman, who has been friends of the family for years came to visit last night. When we told her that we had been listening to you, she got very upset. She said that if we continued to listen to you she would never speak to us again." The family then said that this was the most difficult temptation of all, because this woman was almost like a second grandmother to the children and they loved her very much.

In spite of all this, all of the members of this family continued to progress and were baptized a few weeks later. Opposition need not deter us in any way. It really helps, however, to recognize it when it comes.

Many Approaches To Hiding Truth

The adversary has been about his awful deeds for quite some time. Even though the world changes with the passage of time, men and women remain subject to the same appetites and passions. He has undoubtedly taken a tremendous personal interest in how evil is packaged. He has become quite adept at his dastardly misery-making. He will spare no method. He has learned what works and probably has his followers engaged in looking for areas of vulnerability in anyone he might influence or recruit. His power is significant.

But protection against his influence is provided for in the plan. He can have no influence over us except what we give him. The devil can never make us do it (1 Corin. 10:13). Each of us has the ability to drive Satan, his followers or his influence from our presence. This power is the ability to invite the spirit of the Lord.

"Light and truth forsake the evil one" (D&C 93:37). Where the Spirit of God is, the devil and his followers cannot be. Our ability to invite the Spirit is largely dependent upon our understanding it, how it works and how to do the kinds of things that are inviting to it. There are many ways in which we can invite the Spirit of the Lord into our lives. These are things which we can and should develop (see Chapter Seven).

II. OVERCOMING OPPOSITION

No matter what obstacles the adversary may put in the way, it is still possible for us to overcome opposition and help people find truth.

The Parable of the Tumbleweed

I once heard an example which has helped me throughout the years. I call it the parable of the tumbleweed. There were once two men driving their cars through the desert. One was raised in the city, the other in the country. It was a long stretch of straight road. Both were traveling "near" the speed limit. As the man from the city sped down the highway, to his surprise, an enormous tumbleweed blew into his path. The size of it startled him. He swerved to miss it and his car overturned, pinning him inside.

The man from the country was traveling down the same road, also at a high speed. A large tumbleweed happened to blow into his path as well. But being from the country, and familiar with the nature of tumbleweeds, he simply plowed directly into it. He did

47

not so much as flinch because he knew that in spite of its size, it did not have much substance. As he hit it, the tumbleweed dispersed into thousands of tiny fragments and disappeared in the wind.

The same is true with obstacles in missionary work. As we exercise our faith to bring to pass righteous desires, obstacles will arise. Such obstacles are often very foreboding in their appearance. They quite regularly appear to be the kind that, unless you swerve, will cause you serious problems. The truth is that they are as tumbleweeds to the power of God. No obstacle, no matter how great, is so large as to force the Lord to go around. The key is to rely upon the Lord.

Too often obstacles will arise and because we see no worldly way of overcoming them, we are diverted from our chartered course. Chances are we were correct in assuming that there was no worldly way of overcoming them. But if our desires are righteous, there are always spiritual ways. The answer to opposition is not to give up. It is to dig in our heels and stand firm. It is to push ever forward, with the strength of the Lord. It is to increase our resolve to do the Lord's will.

Keep Building the Wall

In the Old Testament, Nehemiah was inspired by the Lord to rebuild the wall around Jerusalem. As he undertook this, his enemies sought to frustrate his efforts. The way he dealt with opposition in its various forms is a tremendous lesson that teaches us how do deal with any opposition we may face in sharing the gospel.

At first his enemies simply mocked his efforts. "What *do* these feeble Jews?...." (4:2- *italics added*). But this tactic, which was undoubtedly inspired by the devil, failed because "the people had a mind to work" (vs.6). They continued rebuilding the wall.

48

As the enemies saw the walls going up, their second tactic was to threaten to attack and fight Nehemiah and his people. This, as with every evil design, was also inspired of the devil. Satan and Nehemiah's enemies knew that if Nehemiah's people came to fight, they would not be able to build the wall. In response, Nehemiah told his people, "Be not ye afraid of them; remember the Lord, which is great and terrible, and fight for your brethren, your sons, and your daughters, your wives, and your houses" (vs. 14).

Rather than quit building the wall to go and fight, they returned "to the wall, every one unto his work" (vs. 15). They continued building "every one with one of his hands wrought in the work, and the other hand held a weapon" (vs. 17).

When the wall was almost complete, his enemies turned to a more subtle, yet just as potentially hindering tactic. They sent a message to Nehemiah asking for him to come and *talk*, "Come, let us meet together..." (6:2). But Nehemiah's faith and effort were rewarded and the Lord revealed to him that "they thought to do [him] mischief" (vs 2).

His written response to them could well be a motto for all of us when faced with opposition. He said, "I am doing a great work, so that I cannot come down; why should the work cease, whilst I leave it, and come down to you?" Four times, they repeated this tactic. But rather than worry about them, Nehemiah put his trust in God. He prayed, "Now therefore, O God, strengthen my hands" (vs. 9). He knew what was important. He knew from whence his power came. And he knew how to overcome opposition.

Rely on the Lord

When we attempt to do missionary work and obstacles arise in our path, let us meet them head on with faith in the Lord. If we can do so relying upon the power of God, we will find that such obstacles

49

will disperse from before us and be carried away with the wind. The Lord will bless us as we faithfully strive to share His truth with our brothers and sisters. A sister missionary I know demonstrated this kind of faith. We will call her Sister "Barrett."

Sister Barrett had been working with a family for quite some time. There were many problems they had to overcome. After weeks, they received the promised witness of the restored gospel and desired to be baptized. However, they lived in a place where common law marriages were frequent. They had never been legally married, and church policy was that they do so before they could be baptized. It so happened that by the time they gained testimonies and finished the teaching process, Sister Barrett's mission was almost over. They wanted so badly for her to be present at their marriage and baptism. But they thought it would be impossible for them to get married and baptized so soon.

Sister Barrett went to work. The family was interviewed for baptism. The Mission President told her that he could see no reason why they could not be baptized immediately, according to their desires, provided the couple could be legally married beforehand. As she and her companion began to help them gather all of the paperwork necessary to perform a legal marriage, they discovered that they lacked several documents and signatures that could only be obtained in the capital city.

Sister Barrett then called the mission office, which was located in the capital city, and asked the mission secretary to help her obtain the necessary documentation. She was leaving on Monday and nothing was open Saturday. The young Elder responded, "Sister Barrett, it is three o'clock Friday afternoon. Many offices begin closing right now. I don't see any way we can possibly get all of the things you need in time." Sister Barrett's reply was, "Elder, this is something that will mean an awful lot to them and to me. Please do it." The Elder made a valiant attempt.

As he did, things fell into place. Miracles happened. Several very unusual things happened that the skeptic would call "coincidences" but in reality were the Lord moving mountains. The Elder *almost* succeeded. He obtained most of what was needed, but fell short by a signature or two. He called Sister Barrett to report. Before he could even finish, she interrupted firmly, "Elder, I know that this is right. Please try again." He did so, and through another series of miracles all of the necessary documentation was obtained by late that evening.

With great faith and an understanding of obstacles, Sister Barrett had gone ahead and arranged for the marriage to take place the next morning, convincing the one civil authority to do so on a Saturday morning. But there was still another obstacle.

The two cities were hours apart. The problem was how to get the documentation there in time for the ceremony in the morning. To make a long story not quite so long, it happened. It took some direct revelation and the moving of more mountains through the power of faith, but it happened. The couple was married on Saturday and baptized that Sunday. On Monday Sister Barrett finished her mission.

The Lord honors righteous desires that are consistent with His will. He will bless us to the degree that we are willing to pay the price and qualify for those blessings. Opposition may take different forms. Obstacles may seem insurmountable. But with the help of the Lord, miracles are possible.

Chapter 5 - The Message: Learning Truth

I. THE LORD'S WAY

Once people have come in contact with truth, they must learn it the Lord's way.

A Spiritual Conversion

There is much counsel in the scriptures as to how the gospel should be preached. Specifics, such as exactly how the truth is best presented to specific individuals or groups are often revealed to us as we go about our duties. This is called following the Spirit. This is necessary because people are different, and the Spirit manifests itself differently to different people. The actual process of conversion, however, is the same for everyone.

Whether we grow up in homes where the gospel is carefully taught, or we are introduced to it as adults by the missionaries, each of us goes through the same process. In fact, no matter what our situation we will find that conversion and spirituality are dynamic. We can never take our relationship with God for granted. Spiritual gifts are sacred and must be treated as such (D&C 63:64). An additional tactic the adversary often uses, particularly with active members is the idea that, "All is well in Zion; yea, Zion prospereth, all is well..." (2 Nephi 28:21). He would have us believe that there is no need to maintain or improve our relationship with God because we are fine the way we are.

The process of conversion is beautifully simple. It is a process of developing and exercising faith, repenting, making and keeping covenants and learning to live more like the Savior lived. It is also a process of putting off the natural man and becoming a saint through the atonement of Jesus Christ (Mosiah 3:19). It is a process of becoming like Christ (3 Nephi 27:27). It is a process of learning to be "perfect, even as [our] Father which is in heaven is perfect" (Matthew 5:48). Let us examine each of the major aspects of the conversion process through which every investigator and every member continually passes.

Developing and Exercising Faith

The first principle of the gospel is faith in the Lord Jesus Christ (Article of Faith #Four). Faith in Christ is obtained and developed as we **learn truth** (Romans 10:17), and **live it** (Alma 32:27-28, John 7:17, Matthew 7:24-27).

The saving, spiritual truths of the gospel cannot be taught in the same way worldly concepts and philosophies are taught. Intellectual reason and logic alone will, at best, convey part of the truth. Words in and of themselves are wholly inadequate to fully convey the significance and meaning of gospel truths.

The scriptures themselves are even "wrested" to no avail. It was the Savior himself who said, "Search the scriptures; for in them ye think ye have eternal life: and they are they which testify of me" (John 5:39).

Paul taught that it is impossible for the "enticing words of man's wisdom" (2 Corin. 2:4), to convey spiritual truth and build faith. "Eye hath not seen, nor ear heard, neither have entered into the heart of man, the things which God hath prepared for them that love him. But God hath revealed them unto us by his Spirit; for the Spirit searcheth all things, yea, the deep things of God. For what man knoweth the things of a man, save the spirit of man

53

which is in him? Even so the things of God knoweth no man, but the Spirit of God" (vs. 9-11). He continues, "the natural man receiveth not the things of the Spirit of God; for they are foolishness unto him; neither *can* he know them, because they are spiritually discerned" (vs. 14 - *italics added*).

Spiritual truth can only be conveyed spiritually. Whether we hear truth, read truth or witness the application of truth, it is still necessary that the Spirit of the Lord confirm that truth for it to be correctly understood and for our faith to grow. It is the Spirit which communicates with our souls in the most complete sense and enables us to fully comprehend truth in the way God would have us comprehend it.

Section 50 carefully outlines the process of teaching spiritual truth and building faith:

1-   *A messenger is called and set apart* (vs. 13-14).
2-   *The messenger preaches truth* (vs. 17):
 -        *by the Comforter* (vs. 17).
 -        *in the Spirit of truth* (vs. 17).
 -        *by the Spirit of truth* (vs. 17).
3-   *The receiver receives it by the Spirit of truth* (vs. 19).
4-   *The receiver receives it as it is preached by the Spirit of truth* (vs. 21).

As you can see, it is the Spirit that teaches. It is the Spirit that converts.

Though the process of teaching by the Spirit is quite simple, there are many things that can contribute to the overall success of the experience. A missionary can increase his or her usefulness as an instrument in the hands of the Lord by improving his or her ability to preach as outlined above. The training that missionaries receive in the Missionary Training Centers throughout the world and from their Mission Presidents in the field is directed toward helping them develop in these areas. When the gospel is preached in this manner, the results will be three fold.

The messenger and receiver will:

1-   *understand one another,*
2-   *both be edified,* and
3-   *rejoice together* (vs. 22).

When these three things happen, and people begin to act upon what they have understood, faith is generated. The natural result of increased faith is a desire to repent. As our understanding of God and His Great Plan of Happiness increases, so does our love for Him and our desire to serve Him and keep His commandments. This is not a process that happens to a person only once in a lifetime. Rather, it is a process we are all going through continually (Alma 32:29-42).

Repentance

The preaching of the gospel itself is regularly referred to as the act of "crying repentance" (D&C 18:14-15, 34:6, 36:6). Often the confirming, testating witness of the Holy Ghost, as faith is built, will include personal promptings directing us individually as to how to change the way we are presently living our lives and apply gospel truths. This is because living truth is an essential part of really understanding it.

As we change our lives to conform to principles of eternal truth by actually doing that which we have felt is right, our understanding of truth increases and we are blessed. The Savior taught, "If any man will do his will, he shall know of the doctrine..." (John 7:17). It is difficult for investigators to experience a lasting conversion if they only feel the spirit when the missionaries are present.

People must be taught how to invite the spirit into their own lives when the missionaries are not present. To use a popular metaphor, we must teach others how to fish rather than simply give them a fish. We do this as we invite others to live gospel principles and then help them to do so. We, as missionaries, can do much by encouraging and assisting others as they begin to live the gospel.

The process of repentance is often difficult. It does not usually happen overnight. It is something that requires dedication and consistent effort. President Gordon B. Hinckley said, "It is not easy to make the transition incident to joining the church. It means cutting old ties. It means leaving friends. It may mean setting aside cherished beliefs. It may require a change of habits and a suppression of appetites. In so many cases it means loneliness and even fear of the unknown."[8] Missionaries can do much to help their investigators as they strive to begin to live according to the principles of the gospel.

The greatest thing missionaries can do is to help the investigators learn how to draw upon the Lord's help. The Spirit will not necessarily make repentance easy for investigators or any of us, but it will give us the strength and support we need to be able to recognize our sins, change and improve.

Baptism, the Holy Ghost, Enduring

When sufficient faith is built and repentance undertaken, the ordinances of the gospel come into play. The ordinance of baptism allows us to enter into special covenants with the Lord that will provide guidance and direction as we change. Receiving the gift of the Holy Ghost provides us with the opportunity to receive additional help from the Lord through His Spirit. As we

---

[8]   *Ensign*, October 1987, p.5. © The Church of Jesus Christ of Latter-day Saints. Used by permission.

continue to build our faith, repent and live according to the covenants we have made, we begin to qualify ourselves for the blessings of the Holy temple. In the temple, we participate in sacred ordinances, make additional covenants and receive additional blessings that will help us endure to the end.

II. IN MANY SETTINGS

There are many different situations in which truth can be taught and learned.

A Balanced Effort

Missionary work is simply helping our brothers and sisters through this process. It includes the entire conversion process. Anytime we are helping to bring to pass the eternal life of our brothers and sisters in mortality, we are doing missionary work.

Traditionally, missionaries have focused their efforts on finding non-members to teach, teaching them and baptizing them. Recently, however, Church leaders have emphasized that we should "balance" our efforts between the *conversion* of non-members, the *retention* of recent converts and the *activation* of members who have fallen away or become less active. *Service* has been emphasized as something that should happen throughout.

Combining our efforts to convert, retain and activate *simultaneously* will produce greater results than working on each aspect of missionary work separately. Recent converts and less-active members will provide tremendous support and assistance to those who are learning about the gospel. The resulting positive experience will also strengthen the recent converts and inspire those who have been participating less frequently to become more active.

All three of these groups of people will be invaluable sources of new investigators for missionaries. Because as they see the effort put forth by the missionaries and experience the spiritual blessings of participating in the conversion process, their natural desire will also be to share.

On one occasion, two missionaries were introduced to a non-member family with a fifteen-year-old son named "Josh." Josh and his family began investigating the church and were progressing very well. They attended church that first Sunday and had a wonderful experience. As the Elders prayed about how to best help this family progress, they were impressed to solicit the assistance of another fifteen-year-old young man named "Dave."

Dave was already a member of the church, but even though his family was active, he had been less-active for more than a year. The missionaries went to visit Dave. When he heard that Josh and his family were taking the discussions, Dave agreed to accompany them to the next discussion. He was excited that a friend from school was learning about the gospel. As Dave and the missionaries entered Josh's home, there was a brief, teenage-style salutation between the two young men--brotherly and warm--followed by a conversation that went something like this:

Dave: "Hey, I didn't know you were investigating the church? That's great!"
Josh: "Yeah. I didn't know you were a member?"
Dave: "Oh yeah, I've been a member for a long time."
Josh: "Well, I went to church last Sunday and I didn't see you there."
Dave: [long pause] "Well...I haven't been for a little while...*but I'll be there this Sunday!*"

And he was. Not only was Josh (the nonmember), blessed by Dave's presence during the discussions, but Dave (a less-active member), was blessed by the spirit of missionary work and decided to come back to church. But the story does not end here. When other young men at school (also nonmembers), found out that Dave and Josh were both going to church, some of them became interested in learning more about the gospel as well.

Missionary work is contagious. The Spirit that accompanies the work is unlike any other. It is a feeling of profound significance. When you are involved in the work of the Lord in this way and can see the results in peoples' lives, everything else seems to pale in importance.

How to Share Truth

There is much counsel in the scriptures as to how to share the truth with others. One of the most often quoted is the counsel of Alma to his prospective missionary son Shiblon, "Use boldness, but not overbearance" (Alma 38:12). We are also told to go about our missionary work "with [our] might, with the labor of [our] hands...," and that our voice should be "the warning voice...in mildness and in meekness" (D&C 38:41).

At another time, the Lord said we should share "with all humility, trusting in me, reviling not against revilers...." He has said we should "speak freely...preach, exhort, declare...even with a loud voice, with a sound of rejoicing, crying--Hosanna, Hosanna, blessed be the name of the Lord God" (D&C 19:30,37).

One of the most important things to remember, however, is that every ounce of missionary work must be motivated by love. It is difficult for investigators, or others with whom a missionary may work, to confide in someone who serves out of duty or some other reason (Moroni 7:8). The saying, "No one cares how much you know until they know how much you care," is true. If the urgency spoken of in Chapter One is not there, a missionary's words will be hollow. They will sound as "sounding brass, or a tinkling cymbal" would sound in place of the entire orchestra (1 Corin. 12:1). When genuine concern for the spiritual welfare of others is present, the Spirit will be also. One such example happened recently in another part of the world.

A brand new missionary arrived in his first area, quite apprehensive about the next two years. He was shy by nature and nervous about talking with people. His companion was anxious to get him involved in doing the work and help him gain some confidence. As they went about their work that morning, they knocked on a few doors. Each time, the senior companion would invite his new companion to lead out. And each time he declined. After lunch he agreed to make his first attempt.

Knees shaking, he walked up to a door. His companion was behind him providing encouragement. Timidly, he tapped. In his mind, he was reviewing over and over again the words he would say. In an almost violent way, a woman opened the door and practically yelled, "What do you want!" This shy young Elder responded, "Uh, we're missionaries from the Chur....." But before he could finish his sentence she yelled, "We don't want any!" And she slammed the door. The poor missionary was crushed. He did not know if he could handle two years of this. He broke down. But then his companion, a warm and loving young man, put his arm around his new companion, gave him a hug, and said, "It's O.K., sometimes this kind of thing happens. But don't worry. You did a great job. Let's try again. Someone will let us in." And they moved on.

What they did not know, was that once the woman slammed the door, she ran to the curtain to watch the reaction of the two missionaries. When she saw the Elder show concern for his companion, the spirit touched her. She was touched by the love that was shown. A couple of days later, she was out in the yard with her husband. When the two Elders walked by, she called them over and said, "I would like to apologize for the other day.

THE MESSAGE: LEARNING TRUTH

You couldn't have come at a worse time. It seemed like everything was going wrong that day. Would you please come in for some juice?" The two Elders agreed (enthusiastically, of course). Once in the home, they asked if they might present a brief message. A few weeks later, the family joined the church. There is great power in love.

A friend of mine had a similar experience as she began to learn the truths of the restoration. Her friend "Janice" who was the messenger or missionary in this situation, presented truth to her in a way that is often most effective. We could all learn about missionary work and how to share truth from this wonderful woman.

"Kim" and Janice first met when Kim, a widow, moved into the neighborhood. Janice was right there as the family moved in to assist in any way possible. She brought over meals, etc. Janice became aware right away that the gospel could greatly bless Kim's life. She desired so for her to have the truth.

As time went by, Kim found herself presented with several "formal" invitations to learn more about the gospel and to participate in church activities. But she did not feel comfortable becoming involved. These invitations generally came from people she did not know, or from whom she felt she never heard, unless they were inviting her to participate in a church function. She began to wonder whether they cared about her as a person, or as just another convert.

Janice, on the other hand, continued to be her friend. She was always bringing over goodies of some kind, taking care of the family when they were sick, etc. She went out of her way to love and serve Kim and her family. She proclaimed the gospel by her actions. Janice knew that Kim probably would not be interested in learning the truths of the restored gospel until she could see its fruits and feel that others cared.

It is difficult for any one to be the recipient of such acts of love however, and not feel the Spirit. As time went by, Kim began to wonder why any one would do such things and expect nothing in return. She wondered if it might have something to do with her religion. Finally, Kim could stand it no longer. In a tender moment, she asked Janice to explain what motivated her. When Janice confirmed that it was her testimony of the Savior and His gospel and her desire to do as He would do, Kim wanted to know more. She then asked if she could begin attending church with Janice. To make a long, beautiful story short, Kim entered the temple recently for the first time. She has been the recipient of many of the blessings of the gospel.

Notice Janice's approach. Notice that Kim rejected several opportunities to learn more until she had experienced the love and tasted of Kim's light and truth. Then, *she* actually *asked* to be taught more truth. Her desire to learn more and her willingness to accept Janice's invitation were the *natural result* of being spiritually prepared. She was taught truth in a way that was inviting to the Spirit. She did not even know she was being taught. When the time was right, Janice needed simply to bear further testimony and to invite Kim to act upon the feelings of the Spirit. There are so many around us like Kim. Can we be like Janice?

Perhaps the most important point regarding how the work should be done is that *something be done.* "But with some I am not well pleased, for they will not open their mouths, but they hide the talent which I have given unto them, because of the fear of man. Wo unto such, for mine anger is kindled against them. And it shall come to pass, if they are not more faithful unto me, it shall be taken away, even that which they have (D&C 60:2-3)."

One of the greatest needs in missionary work is for us to simply speak up more. This principle will be discussed further in Chapter Seven.

THE MESSAGE: LEARNING TRUTH

One of the main messages of this book is that the Lord can guide our footsteps much better if we are walking. He will only inspire our words if we are willing to speak. If we are willing, there are things that even the least of us can do that can cause great miracles.

Chapter 6 - The Messenger: Weak and Simple

I. THE LORD'S WEAK AND THE WORLD'S WEAK

There is a difference between the world's definition of weak and simple, and the Lord's use of the same phrase.

Weak and Simple?

Karl Marx is often credited with saying "Religion is a crutch for the weak!" The use of this phrase is not unlike the inspired Constitution of the United States being used to justify a ban on the acknowledgement of, or reference to, deity in government-sponsored settings. Those who claim that deference to God is nonsensical, foolish or weak, place themselves in a very dangerous position. They are, in a very real sense, biting the hand that feeds them. "And in nothing doth man offend God, or against none is his wrath kindled, save those who confess not his hand in all things, and obey not his commandments" (D&C 59:21).

Just what do we mean when we say that those who proclaim the gospel are the "weak and simple?" Actually, it is the Lord who used the phrase. "Wherefore, I the Lord, knowing the calamity which should come upon the inhabitants of the earth, called upon my servant Joseph Smith, Jr., and spake unto him from heaven, and gave him commandments; And also gave commandments to others, that they should proclaim these things unto the world.... That the fullness of my gospel might be proclaimed by the weak and simple unto the ends of the world, and before kings and

64

THE MESSENGER: WEAK AND SIMPLE

rulers" (D&C 1:17-24). The Lord is the one who refers to those of us who share the gospel, and even the prophet Joseph Smith as weak and simple.

While most who read this book will not consider Joseph Smith a weak man, he is the very embodiment of this principle. You and I are quite familiar with many of the great and marvelous miracles that have been wrought by the hand of the prophet Joseph. For us, it may be difficult to see Joseph Smith as having been *weak* in any way. But suppose you were born around 1770 and settled in rural New York.

How might you have felt if, at fifty years of age, you heard tell of a fourteen-year-old boy who just emerged from a nearby grove of trees proclaiming that the very God of heaven and His Son, Jesus Christ (never before considered separate beings), had appeared to him? How might you have felt had you heard that this young boy claimed that he was instructed to restore the true church of Jesus Christ, because all of the presently existing churches, including perhaps the one you faithfully attended, were false?

Because Joseph's testimony is true, and the Spirit confirms that it is, you may have been touched by the spirit and interested in learning more. Many were. Even today, the experiences of the young Joseph spark great interest in the hearts of many throughout the world. We have learned to be true to these principles as great tools in proclaiming the gospel. The spirit testifies of them powerfully.

But if you had heard the story after it had been passed along, embellished or distorted you may have brushed it off, or even laughed at the ridiculous antics of a "weak" and foolish boy. You might have supposed a fourteen-year-old boy, with hardly any education, to be obviously too "simple" to do anything of such magnitude. Perhaps this gives you a feeling for how the worldly might feel about the messengers of truth even today.

65

Because spiritual things are spiritually discerned and the "natural man" is incapable of comprehending them, attempts by the worldly to explain them are futile. The whole entire matter of religion and God is irrational and confusing when we deny the inner whisperings of the Spirit and attempts to understand spiritual things in the same context as temporal things. "...They that are after the flesh do mind the things of the flesh; but they that are after the Spirit the things of the Spirit" (Romans 8:5).

I am confident, however, that the reason the Lord refers to His servants as "weak and simple" and the reasons the world may refer to them as "weak and simple" are quite different.

The World's Weak

Sometimes, those who become familiar with part of mortality will assume that they are experts in all aspects. Perhaps it is because they spend so much time in their areas of expertise, that they have little exposure to the beauty and significance of other dimensions of mortal life. In these situations, they may assume that because they have some superficial "understanding" of these other aspects (such as religion), they understand all they need to understand.

Others may have derived what they consider to be tremendous satisfaction from their fields of endeavor. If their accomplishments and efforts have been righteous, they will no doubt have experienced good, positive feelings of fulfillment. It is sometimes more difficult for these people to recognize the need for additional, spiritual nourishment. Wise people, however, have always discovered that as their knowledge increases, there is much more they need to learn.

The Parable of the Pauper

Those who claim they know all they need to know are not unlike the pauper who lived in a shack outside a high stone wall that encompassed many acres of land. He did not know what was inside the wall because it was very high and the only gate remained locked at all times. He had a small garden and with tremendous effort was able to maintain a meager, but sufficient existence.

One day, he was visited by a messenger who was dressed as though he were a servant of royalty. The messenger presented him with a beautiful, solid gold key. He was instructed that the key would open the gate in the wall, and that inside was a large kingdom that he had just inherited from a brother he did not know he had. All he had to do was enter the kingdom and claim it for himself. The pauper, fearing deception, laughed mockingly at his visitor and sold the key for the value of its gold.

Our perspective is often limited by what we have experienced. This is how the spiritually blind see, or rather do not see, spiritual things. They simply cannot comprehend them. Often at the outset, they are unwilling to try. Missionary work is the process of enabling the Spirit to convince them that they ought to at least try the key before selling it.

Gospel truths cannot be understood from mere economic, social, political, practical or other worldly points of view. They can only be fully understood from a spiritual perspective. The fact that someone does not understand something has no bearing on whether or not it is good or true. The fact that many fail to understand the gospel has no effect on its potential to bless them, only upon the likelihood of its doing so. Ironically, it is the very truths of the gospel that enable the world to learn, and thereby develop the molds into which they try so hard to fit spiritual things.

Fortunately, our Father in Heaven is merciful. In spite of our weaknesses and the weaknesses of many of His children who will not see, everything was anticipated and provided for in the plan.

The infinite atonement, wrought by our Savior, can compensate for any amount of weakness if we will allow it to do so. No matter how great the weakness, His mercy and grace are sufficient.

The Lord's Weak

Indeed, the Lord could not use us as missionaries if we did not have these weaknesses. Weakness is a gift that helps us to be humble (Ether 12:27). Only the humble can be sensitive enough to listen to and follow the Lord. This is why He has always used the weak and simple to accomplish His purposes. Paul said, "of myself I will not glory, but in mine infirmities" (2 Corin. 12:5), after experiencing the value of weaknesses.

He was given a physical difficulty of some kind to help him stay humble "lest [he] should be exalted above measure through the abundance of revelations" he had received (vs.7). He "sought the Lord thrice that it might depart" from him. But the Lord said, "My grace is sufficient for thee: for my strength is made perfect in weakness" (vs. 8). Once Paul realized this, his attitude was different. "Therefore I take pleasure in infirmities, in reproaches, in necessities, in persecutions, in distresses for Christ's sake; for when I am weak, then am I strong" (vs.10).

Moroni expressed a similar concern regarding "the awkwardness of [his] hands." He felt that he was not "mighty in writing like unto the brother of Jared" (Ether 12:24). He feared that "the Gentiles [would] mock" at the things he had written (vs. 23). But all such fears discount the power of God. The Lord said, "Fools mock, but they shall mourn; and my grace is sufficient for the meek, that they take no advantage of your weakness" (vs. 26).

The great prophet Moses had a speech impediment. Many of the great leaders in the scriptures were young. Others were uneducated as to the things of the world. Our modern prophets sometimes deal with physical difficulties. This enables them to be more powerful instruments in the hands of the Lord. The way the Lord blesses them is glorious and wonderful. It is unlikely that any one of them would have been as powerful had he not gone through the furnace of trial and tribulation, meeting weakness face to face.

The Fall and Mortality

To our Father in Heaven, anyone in a mortal physical state is subject to weakness. It is one of the great blessings of the plan. The fall, along with the creation and the atonement, is one of the three great pillars of eternity. In it, "all things passed downward to a lower status; they lost the station and dignity that once was theirs and were changed from the primeval and paradisiacal state to their present mortal state. This change from a deathless state brought with it all things that appertain to mortality including procreation, disease, suffering and death. None of these existed on this earth prior to the fall."[9]

Our physical bodies are mortal and therefore subject to weakness. They get tired, they can become diseased and die and they are subject to all kinds of appetites and passions. You may have heard "the spirit indeed is willing, but the flesh is weak" (Matthew 26:41).

In Romans Chapter 8, Paul talks about the struggle between the mortal flesh and our immortal spirits. He tell us that "to be carnally minded is death; but to be spiritually minded is life and peace" (vs. 6). In order to progress and eventually become as God, we must grow by overcoming weakness in the flesh through the Spirit. "If ye through the Spirit do mortify the deeds of the

---

[9]   Bruce R. McConkie, *A New Witness for the Articles of Faith*, Deseret Book Co., 1985, pp. 84-85. Used by permission.

body, ye shall live" (vs. 13). Just like the string to the kite, that which holds us down is also the very thing which enables us to fly. Our weaknesses enable us to progress. They give us something to overcome (2 Nephi 2:11).

To Err is Human

Working as I have for several years in training missionaries I can testify that those who come to the MTC's throughout the world, both young and old, have plenty of weaknesses. Particularly as some attempt to make the transition from a life of selfishness to a life of selflessness, examples of immaturity and a lack of wisdom sometimes emerge.

Though there are some absolutely outstanding exceptions, the vast majority of this great army of the Lord is comprised of young people with generally no college degree, no professional experience and only the social skills that can be developed in high school. Even senior missionaries have their share of weaknesses. Though they have usually learned a lot through the "school of hard-knocks," they sometimes feel they are too old to learn and progress. Some couples find being together constantly for the first time in their lives to be more of a challenge than they expected. Regular member-missionaries also have weaknesses.

Nevertheless, I have had the opportunity of sitting with all kinds of missionaries in different places and observing as they teach and share the gospel with investigators. With very few exceptions, I have seen the same miracle happen over and over again. The Lord takes these weak and simple messengers, both young and old, and transforms them into great and powerful instruments in His hands. With the touch of the Master's hand they become polished arrows in His quiver. Spiritually they reap a great harvest.

Time after time I have seen missionaries do and say things far beyond their own individual capabilities, often without even knowing it. I have also experienced the Lord's interest in the welfare of His children personally. On many occasions, *I* have been inspired to know something, to do or say something or to be somewhere that would make a difference. In those situations, I have often known beyond question that I was being blessed. I have been amazed at how the Lord could do such great things, even through me.

Weakness is Strength

Often new missionaries are more spiritually powerful than some of those who have been serving for a while because they recognize their weakness and rely on the Lord. I remember sitting with one companionship not too long ago and witnessing this very thing.

The senior companion had only a couple months left in his mission. The junior companion had been out for only a couple of months. As the senior companion taught, he taught with humor, interesting stories and examples and a very entertaining demeanor. He was dramatic, he was articulate and he was *very* confident. He seemed to rely heavily on his own experience. I noticed, however, that he did not seem to address the individual needs of the man he was teaching.

His companion, on the other hand, felt intimidated somewhat by the more experienced missionary. The little bit of the discussion he was allowed to teach was not nearly as entertaining. But as he taught, it became evident that, 1) he knew from whence his strength came, and 2) that the message he was sharing meant something to him personally. It was obvious that his intentions were to do the Lord's will and meet the spiritual needs of the individual.

He was not as articulate, but his words seemed to have much more meaning. His testimony was pure and simple. To me, it was infinitely more spiritually powerful than his companion's words.

PROCLAIM MY WORD

There was a spiritual weight to what this second missionary taught that was seriously lacking in the first. The sad thing was that the "senior" companion did not appear to notice the difference.

A couple of months later, the man was baptized. And though the entire family enjoyed the fun-loving nature of the senior companion, guess who the investigator asked to perform the actual baptismal ordinance? That is right. The humble junior companion. I would venture to say that it was *his* humble, yet spiritually powerful, witness that made the most difference in this man's life. He taught, "as one that had authority..." (Mark 1:22).

II. MY GRACE IS SUFFICIENT FOR ALL

The Lord can use each one of us to accomplish His great purposes.

Weaknesses are Gifts

One of my favorite scriptures is Ether 12:27. "If men come unto me I will show unto them their weakness. I give unto men weakness that they may be humble; and *my grace is sufficient for all men that humble themselves* before me; for if they humble themselves before me, and have faith in me, then will I make weak things become strong unto them" (*italics* added).

From this powerful verse, we learn that weaknesses are gifts if we recognize them and humble ourselves. When we begin to feel as though we know a lot or are particularly skilled and talented, we become useless to the Lord. A wise man once said with regard to missionary work, "As soon as you think you can do it by yourself, the Lord will let you." When we are humble and willing to rely on the Lord, spiritual promptings will come. As we follow the Spirit, we become much more powerful tools in His hands. We never know how much influence we can have in a person's life.

THE MESSENGER: WEAK AND SIMPLE

Let me share with you a few examples of people the world might have considered weak or simple, but who accomplished great things with the Lord's help.

A Youth Leader

Missionary work is helping any of our brothers and sisters experience conversion, whether directly or indirectly. I know a youth leader who seemed to always take an interest in the young men of the ward. He was not perfect. He had weaknesses. But he did what he could to see that they fulfilled their assignments, and he helped them set and reach goals.

Brother Art Paulson took a special interest in those that had special needs, particularly those whose families were not active in the church and who needed help and support in that area. He took an interest in one particular young man I know named Steve. Steve's family was less-active in the church. Steve's older brother had gone astray. Bro. Paulson cared enough to see if he could help Steve avoid the same path.

During the week he would make sure that Steve had a ride to and from mutual and Scouting activities. On Sunday he would always stop by with his family on the way to church and pick him up. As a result, Steve participated actively in the church throughout his teenage years. When he turned nineteen years old he served an honorable mission. He went on to earn undergraduate and graduate degrees and have a productive career. He became a good husband, father and grandfather. His children served honorable missions, were married in the temple and are all active and serving in the church.

I wonder if Brother Paulson, this great humble man, a youth leader, had any idea of the extent to which his influence would be felt. For me, the extent of his actions appear to have been significant. He was a missionary in the most complete sense of

73

the word. The young man he took an interest in was my father, Steven R. Littlefield.

Sometimes we seem to take the position that the way we fulfill or do not fulfill our responsibilities as members of the church is our own business. We act as though we are the only ones that are affected by our actions or inaction. But our leaders have made it clear that "God will hold us responsible to the people we might have saved had we done our duty."[10] Our influence is significant in scope. It has far-reaching effects. Whether those effects will be for good or for evil is up to each of us individually. But there will be effects. Indeed, we do not live in a vacuum.

A Prospective Missionary

Another man was a convert to the church. He also had weaknesses. Circumstances were such that he did not serve a mission at the usual age. He was several years older when he began to consider the question seriously. He sought counsel and advice from many sources, but ultimately the decision was his. What complicated the decision was that he was engaged to a beautiful young woman who loved him very much. She was willing to be supportive of him either way. It basically came down to whether or not he wanted to serve. He was of the age that he could have been honorably excused from serving a mission had he so desired.

Many counseled him so to do, but he decided that he had been blessed with so much that the least he could do was spend a short period of his life sharing those blessings with others. He was called and served faithfully, facing some unusual trials and difficulties not faced by most missionaries.

---

[10] John Taylor quoted by Spencer W. Kimball, *Go Ye Into All the World*, 1975. © The Church of Jesus Christ of Latter-day Saints. Used by Permission.

Perhaps it was because he was older, or because he felt particularly strong about what he was doing, but he was *very* successful. I was in a position to know that he was responsible for more than four hundred people entering the waters of baptism during his eighteen- month mission. Several wards and branches of the church now exist, primarily because of his efforts. He was not perfect, he had weaknesses, but he was willing to serve with diligence, humility and faith. Even today, great things can happen through average people if they can learn to rely on the Lord.

One Leader With Vision

I know of a man who was called to serve as a Mission President at a relatively young age. When he arrived in his assigned mission, he discovered that there was one particular area of the mission that had a reputation for being a difficult area. None of the missionaries wanted to go there. Even some of the best would go there and get discouraged. He worked to change the perception of missionary work and success in that area, but to no avail. After some time, he made a bold decision. He decided to take the missionaries out of that area altogether. The members complained, but the missionaries in the mission breathed a collective sigh of relief.

Months later, he sent the word out that he was going to open an area where Brigham Young had baptized forty-five people in thirty days. Which was completely true, by the way.

He began to get letters from missionaries all over the mission who wanted to be the first sent to this new area. He selected two somewhat experienced missionaries and two relatively new missionaries and personally took them to the area. There he met with the members and the missionaries. He explained that by working together, productivity would be enhanced. Within three months it became the highest baptizing area in the mission and remained so for quite some time.

What was the difference? It was one of changed attitude. In addition, it was what the missionaries believed. It was in their degree of faith and vision. It began with their Mission President. In this case, a young leader with great vision made a big difference. That leader was President Thomas S. Monson.[11]

You

Reading these examples of tremendous success will likely cause one of two reactions. Some will have their faith increased and desire to do the same. Others will feel even more intimidated, doubting that they could ever be instrumental in bringing to pass something so monumental. May I remind you that all of these people have one thing in common--they are people. All people have weaknesses.

I mentioned earlier, my experience observing General Authorities. Though they are exceptional people by anyone's standards, even they have weakness. But due to the sacred nature of their call, they wear a mantle that allows them to do things that are beyond their individual strength and ability. This is also true regarding missionaries in the field. The Lord magnifies their efforts. The same is true for any of us who desire to do the Lord's work. He will magnify us as we fulfill our literal responsibility to proclaim His word.

---

[11] See *Inspiring Experiences that Build Faith*, Deseret Book Co., 1994, p. 137-38.

Chapter 7 - The Messenger:
Worthy of Hire

I. FEAR

The Lord can make any of us into useful tools in His hands. Fear, however, gets in the way of our usefulness.

Afraid of What?

Perhaps the greatest obstacle to effective missionary work is fear. Just what is it that we are afraid of? I have asked this question to many members and missionaries over the years. When people are candid, their answers are quite revealing. Some of the responses I have heard often are: rejection, embarrassment, offending someone, sounding fanatical, ending a friendship, being asked a question they cannot answer or sounding like we are more interested in our church than we are people--just to name a few.

As I have contemplated these and other answers, they all seem to stem from one of two things; either a lack of understanding and appreciation for the gospel or a shortage of love for our fellow man. A Ward Mission Leader I once knew seemed to exhibit symptoms of the former.

Two missionaries in a particular mission were both newly assigned to the ward where this man lived. Since he was their primary contact with the members of the ward, they began to work closely with him. Not long after beginning to do so, the two

77

missionaries asked the Ward Mission Leader if he had any friends or relatives with whom they might share the gospel. He abruptly answered, "No, I can't think of anyone. I've been a member of the church for some time now, and I've given the names of everyone I know to other sets of missionaries." The missionaries then invited him to begin praying that the Lord would help him find someone.

As the weeks went by, the missionaries periodically asked the same question. Each time the answer was no. But the longer this man, an attorney by profession, worked with these two young Elders, the more the meaning and spirit of the gospel plan began to unfold before his eyes. He experienced firsthand the change that comes into people's lives as they accept and live the truths of the gospel. He was imbued with the spirit of missionary work, and the power it has to change lives.

Eventually, the missionaries asked the question again. This time, the response was, "Well, there is one family...the `Millers.'" As the missionaries listened, they discovered that the Millers were this man's next door neighbors! They were some of his closest and dearest friends. Both Mr. and Mrs. Miller taught at the local university. They were bright and capable people. Even though the missionaries had asked repeatedly for referrals, it was not until they helped him feel the power of the gospel plan that he felt confident enough to share it with those closest to him.

I have also witnessed examples of the latter. As members, many of us have been asked by faithful leaders and missionaries to exercise our spiritual muscles and share the truth with specific indivuals we care about. Sometimes there are feelings of discomfort when we are asked to stretch in this manner. As we contemplate our love for these individuals, however, our fear is often cast out and we are inspired to action. We are regularly quite surprised at how well our friends and family respond to the truths of the gospel.

Not the Lord's Way

The Lord has given stern rebukes to those who have feared. Through the prophets Isaiah in the Old Testament, and Jacob in the Book of Mormon, the Lord has given this firm command, "Hearken unto me, ye that know righteousness, the people in whose heart I have written my law, fear ye not the reproach of men, neither be ye afraid of their revilings. For the moth shall eat them up like a garment, and the worm shall eat them like wool. But my righteousness shall be forever, and my salvation from generation to generation" (2 Nephi 8:7-8, Isaiah 51:7-8). In these words we are reminded of the eternal nature of the Great Plan. The Lord reminds us that any opposition from man will only be temporary.

David Whitmer was chastened because he "feared man" (D&C 30:1). The Lord commanded him, "And your whole labor shall be in Zion, with all your soul, from henceforth; yea, you shall ever open your mouth in my cause, not fearing what man can do, for I am with you. Amen" (vs. 11). The Lord even reminded the prophet Joseph Smith of this principle on several occasions. He once told him that even "if the very jaws of hell shall gape open the mouth wide after " him, he should "fear not what man can do, for God shall be with you forever and ever " (D&C 122:7-9).

The words of Paul to Timothy begin to explain further why we should not fear. "For God hath not given us the spirit of fear; but of power, and of love, and of a sound mind. Be not thou therefore ashamed of the testimony of our Lord..." (2 Tim. 1:7-8). Here we learn that those of us who have the truth, and the responsibility to share it, will be given the power necessary to do so. We also begin to see the importance of the attribute of love in missionary work.

John taught that "There is no fear in love; but perfect love casteth out fear" (1 John 4:18). When we really care about someone, fear leaves. It seems to become irrelevant. It simply vanishes from our minds. John continued, "He that feareth is not made perfect in love" (also vs. 18).

Fear Cast Out

I remember a young woman in a *Sharing the Gospel* class I taught at BYU who expressed concern regarding her ability to share the gospel with her non-member father. The longer she was away from home, however, the more her appreciation and love for her father increased.

As her love for her father increased, so did her desire for his spiritual welfare. Her love for him cast out her fear, and she approached him with great sincerity. Her father accepted the invitation to listen to the missionaries, was converted by the spirit and baptized a member of the church. A year later, she sent me a card and expressed her joy at being sealed to her family, for time and all eternity, in the Los Angeles temple.

It is this same principle that led Moroni to declare, "Behold, I speak with boldness, having authority from God; and I fear not what man can do; for perfect love casteth out all fear. And I am filled with charity, which is everlasting love..." (8:16).

Moroni also taught plainly one of the most important ways in which we can obtain this kind of love. "Wherefore, my beloved brethren, pray unto the father with all the energy of heart, that ye may be filled with this love, which he hath bestowed upon all who are true followers of his Son, Jesus Christ" (7:48). There is so much power in this principle, particularly as it relates to fear. It is so important that he further taught, "if ye have not charity, ye are nothing, for charity never faileth" (vs. 46).

II. SEEKING TO OBTAIN THE WORD

We become more useful instruments in the Lord's hands as we obtain the word.

Being Prepared

Our love for others will also increase as we better understand the Great Plan of Happiness. Remember again the scripture, "Seek not to declare my word, but first seek to obtain my word, and then shall your tongue be loosed, then, if you desire, you shall have my spirit and my word, yea, the power of God unto the convincing of men" (D&C 11:21). There are several important principles we can learn from this verse.

First of all, we learn that it is important to prepare for missionary service. Second, we learn that we do such preparation by obtaining the word. Third, as we obtain the word we will be able to invite the Spirit. Fourth, the word and the Spirit are "the power of god unto the convincing of men."

The Lord taught the early saints that "if ye are prepared ye shall not fear" (D&C 38:30). This powerful bit of wisdom has blessed the lives of many over the years. In the same verse He says, "I tell you these things because of your prayers; wherefore, treasure up wisdom in your bosoms." This "treasuring up" is an important part of being prepared. To share the gospel effectively, we must be continually obtaining the word. It gives us the understanding and appreciation of the gospel plan that we need to teach with power. It is the primary way in which we prepare for missionary work.

As a teenager, I remember feeling anxiety about whether or not I knew the gospel well enough to be a missionary. I took great comfort in D&C Section 84:85 which reads, "Neither take ye

81

thought beforehand what ye shall say; but...it shall be given you in the very hour that portion that shall be meted unto every man."

I breathed a great sigh of relief because I assumed I was being told that I did not need to do anything. I thought that all I needed to do was go on a mission and the Lord would put the words in my mouth. I thought He would tell me exactly what to say whenever it was needed. The only problem was that I somehow skipped the qualifying phrase in the middle of the verse, "but treasure up in your minds continually the words of life." As soon as I understood this, my preparation efforts changed.

Feasting

I realized that I needed to study the gospel more. I needed to "treasure up" the words. The word "treasure" denotes something of great value, something that means a lot to us. I realized that the "words of life" are the truths of the gospel, found primarily in the scriptures. I finally realized that I needed to "feast upon the words of Christ" (2 Nephi 31:20), and not just nibble. This truth has meant more to me over the years than I have the ability to express. Whether we are full-time, stake or member missionaries, the scriptures will be our most valuable asset. They will be our greatest asset in missionary preparation, in teaching the truth to others and in inviting the confirming witness of the Spirit.

As we feast upon the words of Christ, we are blessed in many ways. For the past few years, I have had the opportunity, in addition to my personal scripture study and my reading with my wife, of listening to at least two General Conference addresses each day. It takes just long enough for me to drive to and from work each day to listen to one talk each way.

Over the six-month period between the annual and semi-annual conferences, I am able to listen to each talk several times. I have come to understand the gospel better and received much personal revelation. This has been a wonderful, additional opportunity for me to feast on the words of Christ. It has greatly blessed my life.

Feasting consists of studying *and obeying.* We should read carefully for a sufficient amount of time to allow the truths to make a difference. We should learn the context of the passages we are reading--who is speaking, to whom and under what circumstances. We should ponder the principles taught. We should think about how to apply these principles in our lives. And finally, we should do so. As we live them, our understanding of them will increase.

All of this requires effort. There is a price that must be paid. As we pay this price, we will discover that we got a really good deal. What we receive will be worth infinitely more than any price we paid for it. The Book of Mormon plays an especially important role in our learning and sharing the restored gospel of Jesus Christ.

The Book of Mormon

President Ezra Taft Benson often spoke of the primary role the Book of Mormon should play in our missionary efforts. He said, "We are to use the Book of Mormon as the basis for our teaching...As we read and teach, we are to liken the Book of Mormon scriptures unto us, `that it might be for our profit and learning'" (1 Nephi 19:23). Further, he said, "anyone who has diligently sought to know the doctrines and teachings of the Book of Mormon and has used it conscientiously in missionary work knows within his soul that this is the instrument which God has given to the missionaries to convince the Jew and Gentile and Lamanite of the truthfulness of our message."[12]

---

[12]   *A Witness and a Warning,* Deseret Book Co., 1988, pp. 1-8. Used by permission.

He also spoke of its importance with regard to missionary preparation. In a Priesthood session he said, "Reading the Book of Mormon is one of the greatest persuaders to get men [and, of course, women] on missions. We need more missionaries. But we also need better-prepared missionaries coming out of the wards and branches and homes where they know and love the Book of Mormon. A great challenge and day of preparation is at hand for missionaries to meet and teach with the Book of Mormon. We need missionaries to match our message."[13]

When I first began teaching seminary, a good bishop gave me an unusual assignment. In addition to my regular calling, I was to arise early and travel to the home of a young man in the ward who was preparing to serve a mission and read the Book of Mormon with him for thirty minutes each morning. At first I thought this was a strange request. The young man came from a very active family who read the scriptures together daily, had Family Home evening, etc. His father even worked for the church in the seminary and institute program.

As the months passed, however, I found that our experience with the Book of Mormon was blessing his life greatly. For some reason, it was easier for him to read and discuss the truths of the gospel. We became good friends. He gained the strength he needed to withstand temptation, served a faithful mission, was married in the temple and is now a wonderful husband and father.

It was also a blessing for *me* to get to know him and for the two of us to feel the spirit together. In addition, *my* understanding of, and appreciation for the gospel increased. My ability to live and teach the truths of the Book of Mormon was also enhanced. I received an additional portion of the spirit each day as I supplemented my regular study with these visits.

---

[13]   Ibid.

As we seek to feast and obtain the word, the Book of Mormon will be our greatest resource in learning the saving truths of the restored gospel. It teaches them in a way that is clear and understandable. It teaches those truths which are most essential for our spiritual progress. But the greatest power of the Book of Mormon is in its ability to invite the Spirit of the Lord. Because it is the most correct of any book, the truth is of the deepest and purest kind. The Spirit testifies readily as we study with real intent.

Appreciating What We Have

As we study, our appreciation of the gospel will also increase. All too often, we lack sufficient appreciation of the significance and magnitude of what it means to have a knowledge of the Great Plan of Happiness here in mortality. Of the billions of our Father's children that have experienced mortality on this earth, very few (comparatively speaking), have had the opportunity to enjoy the blessings of the fullness of the gospel. It is sad, but true, that those of us who have unprecedented access to the fullness are often seriously limited in our comprehension of its magnitude.

The gospel is true. Abiding by its precepts, commandments and laws will bring blessings. Each of us has experienced the blessings of the fullness of the gospel to one degree or another. It has even had a significant effect on those who have been unaware, consciously, of the existence of such truths. One need not look far to see the effects of truth on the world. It is recognizing such effects that is often the problem.

Sometimes we get so caught up in the trees that we cannot see the forest. Other times we train ourselves to see only what we want to see. We can even become accustomed to spiritual blessings and begin to take them for granted. Striving to continually stretch and learn by "obtaining the word" will help us avoid such problems.

85

III. OPENING OUR MOUTHS

Our usefulness increases further as we begin to act.

Making A Difference

Once we are busy obtaining the word, we should begin to open our mouths. Our tongues will then be loosed, and we will be able to do and say the things that will help others experience conversion. All of the stories shared in this book are true. They are about normal people who have sought to obtain the word and then opened their mouths to share that truth with others.

In each case, a significant difference has been made. The difference is not made in numbers or statistics, but in peoples lives. Each number represents someone's relationship with their Father in Heaven. It represents a degree of understanding and vision with regard to the purpose of life here on the earth. It represents the avoidance of sin and transgression and the miserable consequences thereof. It represents joy and happiness where before there was sorrow.

Each of us, no matter how weak, can make a difference. The role of *the messenger* in the conversion process is very significant. Ultimately, each investigator must either reject the truths we teach or accept and apply them. But the way the messenger delivers the message can go a long way toward helping him or her accept and live it. It is said that Elder A. Theodore Tuttle used to say that, "you can lead a horse to water but you cannot make him drink. But you sure can salt his oats!" Let me illustrate with another example from the mission field.

Shortly before I finished my mission, my companion and I came upon an unusual investigator couple. As they met us at the door, they enthusiastically ushered us in. Once we were in, they gathered the family around, and we presented the first discussion. They were very active members of a well-known protestant denomination that considers itself a "charismatic" religion. They said their worship services involved a great deal of "praising, speaking in tongues" and "getting in the spirit." They were polite but not really open to a sincere discussion of truth.

Their curiosity was peaked, however, when we told them that modern prophets and apostles like Peter, James and John now walk the earth. And, it just so happened, that a member of the Quorum of the Twelve Apostles was to visit their city in a couple of days to speak at a Stake conference. We invited them to attend and they accepted. They were not really interested in learning truth. It was obvious to us that they accepted out of curiosity, or perhaps a desire to expose what they felt would only be an imposter. They wanted a story to tell. Nevertheless, we felt like we should take them anyway.

Elder James E. Faust was the presiding authority. For the first ninety minutes they were nervous, fidgeting and muttering back and forth. None of the loud emotionalism they were used to was present, and they were not open to the sweet Spirit that permeated the introductory addresses. As Elder Faust stood to speak, however, something was different. The spirit began to bear witness before he even began speaking. It bore witness of who he was and of his sacred calling. It prepared the minds and hearts of the people for the message he was about to deliver. All of the sudden our "investigators" felt uncomfortable. They quit whispering, sat up in their seats and listened attentively.

Elder Faust spoke through an interpreter. His message was simple. It was not dramatic. It was not recently revealed doctrine. He spoke of the simple, basic truths of the gospel. We watched as their countenances changed from arrogance to humility. At the end of his brief address, he asked the interpreter to sit down and he bore his testimony in Portuguese (which is close enough to Spanish that the native Spanish speakers could understand). As he testified, I noticed tears well-up in the eyes of our guests, as they did in the eyes of many others who were present. Elder Faust bestowed an Apostolic blessing on the country and concluded.

The Spirit that was present was so powerful that after the meeting, we did not want to do or say anything to disrupt it. We simply took the couple home in silence and asked if we could return later that evening to discuss the experience. When we returned, they were completely changed. They spoke humbly. "We don't know anything about you or your church. But we do know this; that man is an Apostle of Jesus Christ! We want to know more." A few weeks later, the family joined the church.

I share this experience because it illustrates the power and influence that each individual messenger can have in the lives of others. It was the power of God that changed their hearts. It was not the power of men. The Spirit came, however, not only because of Elder Faust's sacred and special calling, but also because of the ability which he personally had developed to invite the Spirit of the Lord. That ability had been developed through a lifetime of righteous service and experience (D&C 130:20-21). Each of us should seek to learn and grow in the same way.

It is possible for the messenger to invite the Spirit in such a way that it is very easy for those present to feel the Spirit of the Lord. The scriptures tell us that Nephi taught in such a way that "it were not possible that they could disbelieve his words" (3 Nephi 7:18). The end of this same verse gives us insight into how we can have such power "for so great was his faith on the Lord Jesus Christ...." As our faith in Christ increases, so does our usefulness as tools in the Lord's hands. Each and every messenger can make a tremendous difference.

How We Present the Gospel

As we begin to open our mouths, we should think carefully about what we say, and pray in our hearts that the Lord will inspire us as to how to best present the beautiful truths of the gospel to each individual, family or group. How we present them can dramatically affect how our non-member brothers and sisters respond to invitations to learn more.

As a Mission President, Boyd K. Packer illustrated this point powerfully to a group of missionaries with whom he served.

"We scheduled zone conferences. For each one, Sister Packer baked a three-tiered cake, which she and Sister Bateman decorated beautifully--thick, colorful layers of frosting, trimmed beautifully, and with, `The Gospel,' inscribed across the top.

"When the missionaries were assembled, with some ceremony we brought the cake in. It was something to behold! As we pointed out that the cake represented the gospel, we asked, `Who would like to have some?' There was always a hungry Elder who eagerly volunteered. We called him forward and said, `We will serve you first.'

"I then sank my fingers into the top of the cake and tore out a large piece. I was careful to clench my fist after tearing it out so that the frosting would ooze through my fingers, and then as the Elders sat in total disbelief, I threw the piece of cake to the elder, splattering some frosting down the front of his suit. `Would anyone else like some cake?' I inquired. For some reason, there were no takers.

"Then we produced a crystal dish, a silver fork, a linen napkin, and a beautiful silver serving knife. With great dignity I carefully cut a slice of the cake from the other side, gently set it on the crystal dish, and asked, `Would anyone like a piece of cake?' The lesson was obvious. It was the same cake in both cases, the same flavor, the same nourishment. The manner of serving either made it inviting, even enticing, or uninviting, even revolting. The cake, we reminded the missionaries, represented the gospel. How were they serving it?"[14]

The way we present the gospel makes a big difference in how well it is received. The Book of Mormon, for example, can be presented as a history book detailing some of the customs and events of some of the ancient inhabitants of the American continent. Or it can be presented as a sacred record from God that answers all of the fundamental questions of life and brings happiness and joy into the hearts of all who read it. Which would you rather read?

As we learn to present the gospel effectively and in a manner that is more inviting to the Spirit, we become more effective tools in the Lord's hands. We will also find that many more will respond positively.

Positive Responses

It has always been interesting to me to see people of all backgrounds and circumstances drawn toward truth as it is correctly presented. When given sufficient opportunity--that is, one in which the Spirit can testify powerfully--most of our brothers and sisters here on earth will recognize truth and be drawn towards it. There are many who desperately seek truth. Our challenge is to give it to them in the appropriate way. The following experience helped me obtain this perspective.

I was once with a great senior missionary at a bus station. We were waiting for a bus. While waiting, we noticed a row of taxi drivers waiting for the same bus to arrive so that they could take

---

[14]   *Teach Ye Diligently*, Deseret Book Co., 1979, pp. 227-28. Used by permission.

the arriving passengers to their various destinations in the city. There were eight taxi drivers. We approached the first man. This great missionary said, "Excuse me sir, but do you know who Mormon was?" The man responded, "Yes, I know some Mormons." To which the missionary said, "No, do you know who Mormon *himself* was?" The man said, "Uh, no, I guess I don't."

Missionary: "You don't know who Mormon was?! Mormon was one of the greatest Christian prophets that ever lived. In fact, you might even be a descendent of Mormon. And you don't know who he was?" Taxi driver: "Uh, no, I guess I don't." Missionary: "Well, how would you like two missionaries like ourselves to come by your home and explain to you and your family more about Mormon and the things he taught about Jesus Christ?" To this the man responded positively, and we took down his name and address.

We then approached the next man. After we had introduced ourselves and talked for a moment, the conversation naturally turned toward spiritual things (funny how that seems to happen when you are a missionary). When the time was right, this great missionary said something like, "John, we can tell that you really love your family don't you?" To which this second taxi driver said, "Yes...I do." Missionary: "Would you like to be able to be together with your family throughout eternity?" John: "Yes, I really would." Missionary: "Do you know what you have to do to ensure that it will happen?" John: "No, I don't." Missionary: "How would you like two missionaries, like ourselves, to visit you in your home and explain it to you?" John: "O.K." Missionary: "May we take down your name and address, and they will call on you shortly?" To which he responded positively, we thanked him and moved on.

When we approached the third of the eight taxi drivers, the experience was similar. This time the conversation began with

91

plumbing and ended with a discussion regarding the Book of Mormon. But we ended up with the name and address of another family willing to listen to the truths of the gospel. We continued right down the row of taxi drivers, having similar experiences and obtaining similar commitments. In fact, not one of the eight ever responded negatively in any way...until the last man.

We approached him in a similar way. He seemed interested in the gospel topics we discussed, but when it came to making a commitment to allow missionaries to come by and share more, he respectfully declined. By this time I was not expecting negative responses. We had experienced so many positive responses that it took me a little off guard. But not this great missionary. When others might have tipped their hats politely and considered seven out of eight to be successful, he probed a little deeper.

When he felt the time was right, he extended another invitation. Again, the man respectfully declined saying, "No thank you, I'm really not interested." We were confused because he seemed to be genuinely interested in the things we had discussed. But my companion-for-a-day was not willing to give up. When many missionaries would have exited, he remained persistent--all the while trying to show more and more love and patience toward this man. Finally, when he felt the spirit was right, he invited the man a third time. Again the same response. As I grew more and more uncomfortable, this great missionary showed more and more love and an increased desire to understand and help.

After the man had said no several times, the missionary paused for what seemed like a long time and then said, "You know; I know what you're thinking." To which the man's eyes opened wide and he said, in an almost challenging sort of way, "What?" It was almost as though he were daring my companion to tell him what he was thinking. "You're thinking that you're just a man who loves God, loves his family and is fairly content with his life. You're also thinking that we're here to take something away from you, like your religion. But you're wrong, we're not. We're only here to *add* to what you already have so that you can be *more* happy."

When the man heard this, his countenance changed significantly. He humbly asked, "How did you know that?" The missionary then asked lovingly, "How would you like two missionaries like ourselves to come by and explain it to you?" Taxi Driver: "O.K." Missionary: "Please write your name and address on the back of this card." Which he did and we continued on our way.

Through this experience I learned several things. I learned a lot about how to approach people. But as effective as they were, I learned that it was not the specific approaches he used that made the difference. Rather, it was the gospel knowledge, faith and love with which they were shared. I also learned that people want truth. It surprised me how willing each of these men was to discuss eternal truths, and accept invitations to learn more.

Walls Will Come Down

Even this last man, who appeared uninterested on the surface, was truly interested in learning anything he could that would make him more happy. He actually said no several times before he said yes. He just needed to be convinced that our intentions were to bless his life. He needed to be given a taste of the kind of happiness he could experience through the truths of the fullness of the gospel. Once these two things happened, he lowered the barriers--the walls he had put up to protect himself--and he was receptive.

Many of our Father's children will respond similarly if given equal opportunity. They need to know we care, and they need to be given a taste of what the restored gospel has to offer. This is one reason senior missionaries are often so successful. They have spent a lifetime learning how to show love. To simply be in their presence often gives others a taste of what the gospel can do.

93

They, like most members of the church, are living, breathing testimonies of the truth. Their lives are usually examples of the message they preach. They *proclaim His word* through their actions.

Such examples have contributed significantly to the growth of the church throughout the world. As people are exposed to the truth in love, they are more likely to investigate further. I have yet to meet a regular, ordinary member of the church who cannot do this. It is simply a matter of being willing.

The Lord is all powerful. He can bring to pass incomprehensible miracles through even the least of us. With His help, each and every one of us is "worthy of hire."

Chapter 8 - The Work:
Small and Simple Things

I. THE LORD'S ERRAND

The Lord's work is often accomplished through small, consistent acts of love and service.

Great Things

At Corinth, Paul told his brethren, "For ye see your calling, brethren, how that not many wise men after the flesh, not many mighty, not many noble are called: But God hath chosen the foolish things of the world to confound the wise; and God hath chosen the weak things of the world to confound the things which are mighty" (1 Corin. 1:25-26). Today, as then, those of us who proclaim the true gospel are not always looked upon by the world as "wise" "mighty" or "noble." The natural man may consider us "foolish" or "weak."

The Lord sees us differently, however. He has always used what the world would consider "small" means to accomplish great things (1 Nephi 16:26-29, Numbers 21:6-9, John 9:7). "By small and simple things are great things brought to pass; and small means in many instances doth confound the wise. And the Lord God doth work by means to bring about his great and eternal purposes; and by very small means the Lord doth confound the wise and bringeth about the salvation of many souls" (Alma 37:6-7).

Small means can also mean the so-called "little" acts we perform. It was not a difficult and foreboding challenge to read the Book of Mormon with my young friend every day. It simply required a little diligence and patience. Nor was it a tremendous feat for that senior companion to put his arm around his new companion and encourage him. It just took a willingness to make a difference.

It is sometimes easy to feel like missionary work is overwhelming. We may, for example, hear stories of people who seem to "do and say everything right." It seems only natural that such people would have success in sharing the gospel. As we hear converts share their conversion experiences, we sometimes hear of "great things" that the messengers or missionaries did to help them experience conversion. Often these things seem beyond our abilities. We think that because we have never experienced such things, we will likely never be able to.

Let us never forget that this is the Lord's work. We have chosen to participate in His wondrous plan. We have been blessed with the truth. Therefore, we have the opportunity and responsibility of sharing it with others. This opportunity and responsibility is very sacred. As we attempt to do His work we are, in reality, His representatives. All great things that happen to people as they are converted, happen because of the Lord.

No mortal has ever converted another on his own. It is true that two people can do anything if one of them is the Lord. He does not require us to do impossible, superhuman feats. Often it is the little things. A lot can get done if we just consistently do something "small."

Take home and visiting teaching for example. You may think that unless you have some sort of dramatic, earth-shaking experience during each visit, you are not making a difference. In reality, brief spiritual messages, delivered regularly, will have much more of a powerful, lasting effect. It is like eating pizza. Most of us would rather eat one pizza a week for ten weeks than ten pizzas at once. The same is true with missionary work. Consistent doses of spiritual truth can cure big spiritual diseases.

Years ago, when called as a Ward Mission Leader, I discovered that there was a tremendous amount of work to be done. My wife and I had four very small children, and I was having trouble juggling it all. At first I was overwhelmed. I discovered two things that really helped.

First, I realized I did not have to do everything myself. The Lord has organized His Church in such a way that there were always others to assist. Second, I learned I could get a lot done if I were to just do a little, on a regular consistent basis. I learned to keep my priorities straight, and that if I did, I would be provided with the time necessary to do the things I felt needed to be done. It was amazing to me how much could get done little by little.

Imagine how much work would get done if each of us did just one little thing each week--perhaps a visit, a note, a message, a testimony or an act of service. After one year we would have performed fifty-two acts of Christlike love. That is a lot of missionary work! By consistently doing small and simple things like these, great miracles are brought to pass.

Called To Serve

Sometimes callings seem small and simple--almost insignificant. After all, everybody has one. Yet callings are very significant. When a person receives a calling, of any kind, he or she receives a stewardship. With every stewardship is granted the right to receive all of the revelation and help from God which will be needed to fulfill that stewardship. "Therefore, let every man stand in his own office, and labor in his own calling...the body hath need of every member, that all may be edified together, that the system may be kept perfect" (D&C 84:109-110).

97

In missionary work, we are called to be "hunters" and "fishers of men" (Jeremiah 16:16). In ancient times fishing was done primarily with nets, gathering in large numbers at a time. Some of us are called and then assigned to areas where many people are experiencing conversion. In a sense, we cast out our nets and many will be gathered in. As "hunters" we tend to bring them in one by one--to "hunt them from every mountain and from every hill, and out of the holes of the rocks" (also vs.16).

As we have discussed, every member of the church has been given the responsibility of sharing the gospel with others. It is part of the covenant we make at baptism. We promise to "bear one another's burdens, that they may be light," and to "stand as witnesses of God at all times and in all things, and in all places that ye may be in, even until death" (Mosiah 18:8-9).

When a person receives a call and is set apart as a missionary, that person thereby receives additional responsibility, above and beyond that of the regular member. He or she then has unique access, for a season, to an additional portion of the Spirit of the Lord to help accomplish such an assignment. Many returned missionaries will tell you that at first they do not always notice this special help from the Lord. This is because it comes quietly. But they will also tell you that when they are released, its absence is obvious.

Some have sought to take upon themselves this calling and authority. In D&C Section 11 we learn that "you need not suppose you are called to preach until you are called" (vs. 15). Occasionally, on the steps of the United States Capitol building, for example, one can find individuals attempting to "call the country and its leaders to repentance." Most of them feel they have been "called" by God to do so. I have asked some of them, on occasion, to explain how they were called. Their answers vary, but are always in sharp contrast to the way calls are extended in the church.

As with the priesthood, no one "taketh this honor unto himself" (Hebrews 5:4). For it is, indeed, a great and sacred privilege. "Behold, mine house is a house of order, saith the Lord God, and not a house of confusion" (D&C 132:8).

When we have "desires to serve God" we are "called to the work" (D&C 4:3). If circumstances are appropriate and it is the Lord's will, we can be called as full-time missionaries--official representatives of the Lord and His church--twenty-four hours a day, for a period of months. Those who have desires to serve full-time missions can be recommended by their bishops to the brethren for consideration. As inspired by the Lord, the prophet may then extend a call.

The Lord will often use us if we are worthy and willing. But whether we have specific desires to serve and are called as full-time missionaries or not, missionary work is a commandment and opportunity in which *each of us* should be anxiously engaged.

Anxiously Engaged

Another of my favorite scriptures has a great deal to do with agency. "For behold, it is not meet that I should command in all things; for he that is compelled in all things, the same is a slothful and not a wise servant; wherefore he receiveth no reward" (D&C 58:26).

Some of us will rationalize away the fact that missionary work is a responsibility we all share by claiming that we have not been officially called. In doing so, we forget our baptismal covenants and turn a deaf ear to the prophets of God. Others of us will wait for personal invitations, perhaps from church leaders or missionaries to encourage us to do something. In this scripture, the Lord calls this "slothfulness" and says that it "receiveth no reward."

The scripture continues, "Verily I say, men should be anxiously engaged in a good cause, and do many things of their own free will, and bring to pass much righteousness" (vs.27). How much of a difference would it make if each of us were to take this simple commandment to heart with respect to missionary work, if each of us were to take the initiative and anxiously engage ourselves in sharing the gospel with those around us? How much "righteousness" would we bring to pass?

For the Power Is In Them

Perhaps my favorite part of Section 58 is verse 28, "*For the power is in them*, wherein they are agents unto themselves. And inasmuch as men do good they shall in nowise lose their reward" (*italics* added). If there is one message I would like to convey loud and clear with this book, it is that the laborer *is* worthy of his hire (D&C 34:38). The power *is* in each of us to bring to pass great things.

We need not be perfect. We need not be unusually skilled or knowledgeable. We need not be given an additional, special calling. No matter who we are, we can do missionary work. Each of us has the ability within us to share the gospel. All we have to do is be willing to do something, and then do it.

II. THRUSTING IN THE SICKLE

To get started, we need to simply begin sharing.

Where Do We Begin?

There are so many ways in which we can begin. We have already mentioned *service*. Acts of service, motivated by love, teach truth. In addition, such experiences often lead to opportunities to share *scripture* and *personal testimony*, which are most inviting to the Spirit. As people feel the Spirit, we should invite them to act upon those feelings and live specific truths of the gospel. This will invite the Spirit into their lives even more. We should then do all we can to help them as they strive to keep such commitments.

Sometimes our relationship with someone is such that we can just strike up a conversation about sacred things. Other times there is much that will need to be done before a conversation about the truths of the gospel can take place. Even in situations where there is much preparation that needs to take place, we can do much to expose people to truth, thereby allowing the Spirit to testify. Often, just having contact with these individuals will provide them with an example of the gospel influence in our lives. I remember an amusing experience to which you will probably be able to relate.

Years ago, I was invited to attend an inter-denominational conference in Seoul, Korea. It was sponsored by a religious organization interested in bolstering its image among members of other faiths. The incident happened as we arrived in the hotel that first afternoon.

My traveling companions (also church members) and I entered the lobby and were greeted by the host of the conference. He was an outgoing gentleman from the south. He was warm and cordial to all of the participants as they arrived. But when we walked in, his face seemed to light up; and he approached us enthusiastically. We were dressed casually for the long flight (the seminar did not actually begin until the following morning).

With great enthusiasm he said, "You all must be Mormons?" We responded, "Yes sir, we are. How did you know?" "Because you just shine! I can always tell Mormons, because they just shine!" The way we live our lives can be one of our greatest assets in sharing the truth with others.

But sharing the gospel is also possible with those who appear to be far from ready to recognize its benefits or accept it. A young couple I know demonstrated this fact.

They had just moved into a new subdivision. As they began to get to know each of the other new families, they became acquainted with one particular man who was noticeably different. We will call him "Jack."

Jack's life had been bitter. He had spent years at sea and been a party to many evils as he traveled from port to port. After many years, he married a beautiful woman from the Far East and decided to take the money he had saved and settle down. He decided to settle in Utah because of the reputation it had for being quiet and free from crime. He made it very clear from the beginning, however, that he had negative feelings toward the church. He did not really offer any explanations. He simply said he did not like anyone or anything "Mormon."

On the surface he seemed very rough. He did things that many found offensive. Some did not like him at all. Our young member couple knew that if they were going to share the gospel with this man they were going to have to proceed carefully.

Jack loved to talk. But he was used to complaining. It seemed he always felt he was being treated unfairly by someone. The first thing this member couple did was to try and help him complain less. It was not conducive to the Spirit. In their "over-the-fence" conversations, they would do whatever they could to change the tone from negative to positive. Sometimes they succeeded. Other times they just had to end the conversation.

The sister (member-missionary), showed great empathy. She tried to let him know that, in spite of his past, he was still a good person. On one occasion, out by the mailbox, she told him so. His heart was touched and for a moment, he softened. He got tears in his eyes and said "Do you really think so?" It was difficult for him to believe. The sister also went out of her way to serve Jack and his family. Even though she had small children, she would find time to do little things that showed she cared. She would bake goodies, run errands for the family, talk with his children, etc.

As time went by he had good and bad days. Some days they felt like Jack was really making progress. At other times they felt like they might be wasting their time. But as they prayed to know how to help him, something happened that provided a window of opportunity.

Jack was attempting to dig trenches for a sprinkling system, and he hurt his back. This member-missionary couple knew he was anxious to finish the sprinkler system but could not find anyone to do it. The brother notified the Elder's quorum, and several showed up to help (miracle number one). He also notified the full-time missionaries, and they also came to provide service. None of those who helped would accept payment for their services. All were very agreeable as they worked.

This impressed Jack. In fact, it impressed him so much that he arranged for his wife to make oriental cuisine for a Relief Society homemaking activity. He invited the missionaries over for dinner. The missionaries proceeded carefully, and months later Jack's family joined the church. Service is always a good place to start. When love is demonstrated through sincere service, the feelings of the Spirit are often present.

As we serve, we should remember the conversion process. We should always keep in mind exactly how people experience lasting conversion. It is not usually through sports, plays, activities or even fancy, multi-media presentations that sometimes focus on people's emotions. Activities and resources such as church-produced media, can aid in teaching truth, preparing people's minds and hearts. But the important thing to remember is that people need to be exposed to the lasting, saving truths of the restored gospel. These are what will enable them to fully partake of the atonement of Jesus Christ (see chapter Three).

These truths must be presented simply and clearly so that the Spirit can testify of them. As missionaries teach discussions, they rely heavily on the *scriptures* and *personal testimony* because they often do this best.

Many Ways To Serve

Each of us has talents. Each of us has the ability to touch the lives of those around us. As we prayerfully ask, the Lord will provide opportunities for us to use those talents. Another inspired Bishop charged brother "Thomas" with the assignment to activate brother "Jones," a man who had been less-active for years. The Bishop had brother Thomas assigned as a home teacher to the family, and instructed him to do all he could to get brother Jones and his family to the temple.

The only way brother Thomas could make contact with brother Jones was to catch him out in his garden in the early hours of the morning. Brother Jones loved gardening. He was polite but hesitant as home teacher Thomas "dropped-by" early in the mornings. Appointments were scheduled, but brother Jones was never present during the visits. Brother Thomas was only able to teach the semi-active sister Jones and children. Brother Thomas sought the Lord's help and prayed fervently.

After several months, brother Thomas was asked to participate in a ping-pong tournament with the young men of the ward. The fifteen-year-old son of brother Jones also participated. Brother Thomas won the championship with ease.

THE WORK: SMALL AND SIMPLE THINGS

Well it just so happened that brother Jones also loved ping pong. During the next early morning garden conversation, brother Jones asked brother Thomas, "I hear you play ping pong?" Thomas: "Yes." Jones: "Well, I have a table downstairs. Next time you come over, maybe we can have a lesson and then go downstairs and play a game?" Brother Thomas agreed, and to his surprise brother Jones was present during the next home teaching visit.

They all felt the spirit during the brief lesson. Afterward, brother Thomas proceeded to vanquish this new ping-pong opponent as well. To this brother Jones responded, "I know someone who can beat you--my father!" Grandpa Jones was in his seventies. "The next time you come, I want to see you play Dad."

Well, a month later, another inspiring message was presented and the spirit was felt. Grandpa was also present. Afterward, grandpa Jones proceeded to trounce the heretofore undefeated brother Thomas in ping-pong (to the glee of all present)! In the process, a relationship was established. The home teacher seemed to have no trouble teaching the entire family thereafter. *Scriptures* were shared, *personal testimony* was borne, and the two men became better and better friends.

In fact, brother Thomas, a school teacher by profession, was building a shed in his backyard. He would work on it in the evenings after school. No sooner would he begin each evening, than brother Jones would show up, hammer in hand, ready to help. Brother Jones' church activity increased. And in time, all were eventually present together in a beautiful sealing room in the temple. The process took three years.

I Will Go Before Your Face

The Lord's willingness to assist us is much greater than most of us understand. Perhaps it is partly because He knows just exactly how futile our efforts would be without His help (Mosiah 2:20-

105

21). He has given a promise to missionaries that, in and of itself, ought to inspire each of us to action in missionary work. He has said, "...for I will go before your face. I will be on your right hand and on your left, and my Spirit shall be in your hearts, and mine angels round about you, to bear you up" (D&C 84:88).

There is nothing magic about doing missionary work. It is often the simple little things that change people. The most important thing is that we *do something* and that, as we do so we seek the Lord's help. It is as we do these small and simple things that the Lord can bless us and bring to pass great and marvelous things.

Chapter 9 - The Work:
Great and Marvelous Things

I. THE MOVING OF MOUNTAINS

The kinds of miracles that can take place as we take the initiative to do small and simple things are marvelous.

Mountains are literally moved on a regular basis. They are often moved quietly, without pomp and circumstance. But they are nonetheless moved. They are often moved shovelful by shovelful, over a period of time. But they are nonetheless moved.

In missionary work, one can see mountains moved almost daily. I share the following personal experience from the missionfield because I think it illustrates well the moving of mountains, and it gave me a new vision of the Lord's power and His interest in blessing His children. Many of the principles we have discussed are illustrated.

Looking Forward With An Eye of Faith

One morning, my companion and I were studying the topic of faith in the Book of Mormon. As I read Alma 32:40-41, the words, "looking forward with an eye of faith to the fruit thereof," stood out. I sat and pondered them for several minutes. I remembered having discussed them in a zone conference.

I remember thinking to myself that "looking forward with an eye of faith" must mean something like picturing in my mind my investigators being baptized. I immediately got out my goal sheet and made a new goal. I wrote, "I will picture in my mind, the very next family I find, being baptized. I will then do everything I can to make it become a reality."

We finished our study and went to our morning appointments. The first family we taught was on the third discussion and already had a goal to be baptized in a couple of weeks. As we finished the discussion they said, "By the way Elders, we are moving." We said, "Oh no! . . . When?" And they said, "tomorrow." We took down their new address so that the missionaries in the town where they would be moving could pick up where we left off.

Then we did something that missionaries always do when finishing a discussion. We asked, "Who do you know that needs to know what we have been teaching you?" They knew we were going to ask that question because we asked it every time we visited them. But we were especially interested now. The father responded, "Well, there is one man." And we said, "Who?" "My father." We said, "Great! What's his name?" "Don Pedro."

Don Pedro

As soon as he said "Don Pedro" I was concerned, because we knew him. Don Pedro was a prominent citizen. He used to be the protestant preacher of the town. He preached for many years, but was now retired. People in that town thought of him as "the wise old man that lived on the hill."

Nevertheless, we said, "Great! We'll go teach him. When would be a good time?" He said, "I've already told him that you will be by sometime this afternoon." We said that would be fine, and immediately the goal I had made that morning popped into my mind. I did not think anything of it, and we left.

That afternoon we climbed the hill to Don Pedro's home. As we approached the door, a young mother and her children were leaving. When we entered we found that he had just been teaching them parables. I was intimidated, because I was a fairly new missionary myself and my knowledge of parables in the Bible was somewhat limited. But we began the discussion.

He was kind enough to let us pray and was very cordial--until we began teaching. By the time we finished teaching the first principle of the first discussion he had interrupted several times and attempted to contend over points of doctrine. He would show us scriptures in the Bible that he felt contradicted what we were teaching, and then he would proceed to tell us "*the way it is.*" We knew we should not contend. We wanted to maintain a trusting relationship. We also knew that we had been called to teach, and not to be taught (D&C 43:15). Still, all we could do was teach each principle, bear our testimonies, and then listen patiently to his rebuttal.

A Mountain

He was unwilling to seriously consider the truths we taught. It seemed as though all he wanted to do was hear our beliefs, and try to prove them wrong. It was an awful experience. We felt quite discouraged as we left. Nevertheless, at the end of the discussion we did feel like we should say, "Don Pedro, we would like to come back and visit you again if that would be all right?" "Great!" he said. Not unlike a victor having just been challenged to a rematch.

As we walked down the hill, silently hanging our heads, guess what came to my mind? That's right, the goal I had made that morning. I tried to ignore it, but I could not. I thought to myself, "No way, Don Pedro doesn't count!" But the thought persisted. Finally I gave in, and tried to picture Don Pedro being baptized. It was *not* easy. But after a few minutes, I was able to picture it somewhat. Then a thought came to my mind. Somewhat selfishly I thought, "If Don Pedro were to get baptized, imagine what that would do to the members in this area. They would be so convinced of our ability as missionaries, that they would give us the names of everyone they knew. We would never have to knock on another door again!" I began to become interested.

I thought to myself, "This is great! I'm going to do it some more!" I began to picture Don Pedro's baptismal service. As I did, another thought came into my mind. As I pictured the baptismal service, I thought to myself, "If Don Pedro got baptized, the whole town would want to know why he joined the Church. He would be a great asset to the missionary work in this area."

As I thought about these things, I began to smile and my companion asked, "Why are you smiling?" By this time I had really done some "looking forward." I said, "You know what companion? I can picture Don Pedro standing up in front of the Elders' Quorum and saying, `When the missionaries first came to me, I gave them such a hard time. But little by little, they kept coming back, and now look at me, I'm a member of the church.'" I thought my companion was never going to stop laughing.

A few days later we went back for the second discussion with Don Pedro. It was worse than the first. He had dug up some pamphlets written to destroy the faith of those investigating the Church, and attempted to discuss them. Again, all we could do was teach a principle, bear our testimonies, and listen to him ramble. It was awful!

However, as we taught, it surfaced that our understanding of being "saved by grace" was significantly different than that of popular protestant religions. At the end of the discussion he asked, "Well, if you don't believe in being saved the way we do, then what do you believe about salvation?" To which we responded, "We will talk about that tomorrow."

Being Prepared

We spent hours reading everything we could find about salvation, and we prepared a wonderful little lesson entitled, "What we believe about salvation." When we returned again to teach Don Pedro, the visit was different. Since he asked the question, he was not as inclined to interrupt. He just sat there with a skeptical look on his face. When we finished the discussion, he asked, "What's this you said about apostasy?" To which we responded, "We'll talk about that tomorrow." That night, we went home and proceeded to spend some time studying everything we could find on apostasy.

We returned the following day, Saturday, and our experience was very similar to the second. He did not argue because he had asked the question. "Looking forward," we continued to picture him becoming converted. At the end of the discussion, the Spirit said, "Invite Don Pedro to the District Conference tomorrow." I thought to myself, "No, Spirit! Don Pedro is an old man. The District Conference is four and a half hours away on a dirt road. We'll be traveling in the back of a cattle truck because the people are poor and can't afford a bus."

But I continued to feel impressed, so I said, "Don Pedro, would you like to go to the District Conference with us tomorrow?" He said, "What's that?" I said, "It's a big conference at which many members of the church will be present, and we will have a special speaker." "Who's going to speak?" he asked. "Our Mission President," we responded. To our surprise he said, "Oh, your boss, I'd love to go."

The Lord's Blessings

Needless to say, we were shocked. But the next morning, at four a.m. when we pulled up in front of Don Pedro's house with all the branch members in a cattle truck, there was Don Pedro, his wife, and nine of their children. We loaded them all up in our truck, and went "over the river and through the woods" or should I say "through the river and over the woods" to the District Conference.

It was a wonderful trip. Half-way through, it began to rain and we had to pull the tarp over our heads so we would not get wet. We also got quite dusty. But we arrived at the conference just as it was beginning. You should have seen the Mission President's eyes as we walked in with seventy-seven people from a branch of sixty-six members!

I watched Don Pedro carefully. At first, he did not seem very interested. But as is true for all Mission Presidents, ours was a very inspired man. As he spoke, Don Pedro began to listen intently. I will never forget the feeling I had as he spoke. It was as if he had been present during each of our visits with Don Pedro. He spoke with power and authority, and he "just happened" to speak about every point of doctrine Don Pedro needed to hear.

The trip home was long and silent as we pondered the words we had heard and rested from the days activities. That night we visited Don Pedro to get his impressions of the conference. The moment we saw him, we knew. He had felt the Spirit of God, and his heart had been touched. He wanted to know more about what we believed, he wanted to read the Book of Mormon. Three weeks later he was baptized a member of the Church of Jesus Christ of Latter-day Saints.

The most touching part of the whole experience for me, however, happened several months later. I had long since been transferred to another area. I received a special letter. It was from one of the Elders who was then serving in Don Pedro's town. It read something like this:

> "Elder Littlefield, Don Pedro is such a good member. You must have had a hard time teaching him though. Yesterday he stood up in sacrament meeting and

said, `When the missionaries first came to me, I gave them such a hard time. But little by little, they kept coming back. I went to the District Conference. And then, I read the Book of Mormon. And now look at me, I'm second counselor in the branch!'"

As a young, inexperienced missionary, I learned many things from that experience. I learned that the Lord blesses those who serve him and exercise faith. I learned the vital role of the spirit in the conversion process. And I also learned the importance of having a good knowledge of the gospel. But foremost, I learned that the Lord can move what may appear to be even the largest of mountains.

A Missionary

I tried to keep in touch with Don Pedro, but his letters quit coming. When I had been home several months, I received a letter from some of the members in that little town informing me that Don Pedro had passed away. I was shocked. For some time I could not understand why Heavenly Father did not preserve his life so that he could be a great missionary in that town. I pondered this for months, and then one day it came to me.

Many times after coming in contact with the fullness of the true and everlasting gospel, he had commented how much he would have loved to serve a mission and preach the whole truth. Then, it came to me. Don Pedro had been called on a mission. None of his ancestors were members of the church, and he had spent his entire mortal life teaching bits and pieces of the truth to many people. The Lord was giving him the opportunity to teach the true gospel of Jesus Christ to those who had passed on. Let us be careful not to underestimate the Lord's power. Who knows what mountains can be moved if we just strive to exercise faith.

II. FAITH

Faith moves mountains.

The prophet Joseph Smith taught that faith "is the moving cause of all action, the first great governing principle which has power, dominion, and authority over all things."[15] It is so fundamental to our sharing of the gospel. We must better understand and live by it. There are some principles of exercising faith that are particularly important in missionary work. The following example illustrates a few that were helpful for two missionaries.

An Opportunity

Elders Flores and Vilorio, both from Honduras, had just returned from the Mexico City Missionary Training Center. They would both serve their missions in their own country. After a wonderful day of orientation by their Mission President, they lay in their beds that night talking.

Elder Vilorio, who was from a town up north called La Ceiba, said to Elder Flores, from Tegucigalpa, "Tell me about yourself. How long have you been a member?" Elder Flores said, "All of my life...at least since I was eleven." "How many in your family are members of the church?" Elder Flores responded, "All of them." "All of them?" "Well, everyone except my grandmother, and she insists she's going to die Catholic."

"Wow, that must be great! I can't imagine that!" said Elder Vilorio. "Yes, it is great," said Elder Flores. "How about you, how many members are there in your family?" "Just a few." "Well, how long have you been a member?" "One year."

---

[15]   *Lectures on Faith,* compiled by N.B. Lundwall pp. 7-12.

THE WORK: GREAT AND MARVELOUS THINGS

Commitment

At that point Elder Flores, on the first night of his mission, looked Elder Vilorio in the eye and said, "I promise you that if I ever get sent to La Ceiba, I will baptize the rest of your family!" Elder Vilorio, impressed with the faith, responded politely and they went to sleep. The next morning the two had their interviews with the Mission President to receive their first area assignments. Elder Vilorio was sent somewhere to the south. But guess where Elder Flores was sent? That's right, to La Ceiba.

Work

After a couple of weeks Elder Vilorio got a letter from Elder Flores that went something like this, "Dear Elder Vilorio, we've met your family, and they are very nice people. They've agreed to let us teach them the discussions." Elder Vilorio wrote back, "That's great. I'm really glad you will be able to teach my family the discussions. Do you know how many sets of missionaries have taught my family the discussions?"

A week or two later Elder Flores wrote again, "Elder Vilorio, we have been teaching your family, and they are progressing well. In fact, they have a goal to be baptized on [such and such a date]." Elder Vilorio wrote back, "*Good*. Do you know how many goals to be baptized my family has had?" Elder Flores' next letter said, "Elder Vilorio, we just baptized your family!"

More Commitment

Overwhelmed with joy and after thanking the Lord on his knees for this great blessing, Elder Vilorio wrote back, "Elder Flores, I promise you that if I ever get sent to Tegucigalpa, I will baptize your grandmother!"

115

Well, the next time missionaries were reassigned areas, guess where Elder Vilorio was sent? That's right, Tegucigalpa. After a couple of weeks the letters began again, "Elder Flores, I met your grandmother and she has agreed to let my companion and me come by and teach her." Elder Flores wrote back, "*Great.* Go right ahead. Do you know how many times the missionaries have taught my grandmother?"

More Work

A few more weeks passed by, and Elder Flores received another letter, "Elder Flores, we have been teaching your grandmother and she has a goal to be baptized on [such and such a date]." Elder Flores' response was the same, "That's really nice Elder Vilorio. Do you know how many times my grandmother has set a goal for baptism?" And then came the final letter, "Elder Flores, we just baptized your grandmother."

Meaning It

As wonderful as these two elders were, they were not perfect. The Lord blessed them because their hearts were in it. This qualified them for a His help. They also *believed* that He would help them. They relied on the Lord. They had genuine love and exercised faith in Him. They really meant to bless each other's lives, and they obeyed the principles of faith that allowed the Lord to bless them with such great miracles (D&C 130:20-21). *Commitment* and *work* are two such principles.

There are many such examples of miracles in missionary work. Miracles happen when true principles are obeyed. Faith can be exercised in different situations and by different people, but the principles governing it remain the same. As we learn those principles and apply them, great things happen.

THE WORK: GREAT AND MARVELOUS THINGS

A Neighborhood Effort

"Dan," was orphaned as a young boy. He and his brother were passed around from relative to relative. As a result, they lacked the security that children need and began to get into trouble. His only exposure to religion was through a foster family. It had not been a positive experience. By the time he was in high school, he had done much of the wrong there was to do. His life continued on this path for several more years.

At his ten year high school reunion, he met a former female classmate we will call "Denise." Dan was interested in her, but Denise, a member of the church, would not have anything to do with him because of his lifestyle. When he persisted, she told him that the only way she would even consider going out with him is if he were to clean up his act. He did, and after some time the couple was married. Years later, they built a home in our new neighborhood.

Dan stood out as a nonmember. He had long hair, rode a Harley Davidson motorcycle and played in a rock band. He was nervous about how people would perceive him. He came from California and wondered if people in his new Utah neighborhood would be as tolerant.

At first, he felt as though only a few people would even speak to him. He felt uncomfortable. But he went out of his way to be nice to people. It did not take long before he began to become friends with many on the block.

As they became friends, several of his neighbors wanted to introduce Dan to the gospel. Wisely, most felt a greater need to become his friend first. He had made a lot of progress in recent months and was very surprised that he had come so far. He had given up many things that were not compatible with a good family life. Yet, he was very tentative about the future. He did

117

not know if he could maintain such a lifestyle permanently. A couple of people invited him to church, etc. but he politely declined. It seemed too overwhelming.

Oh, the wonderful things that then happened! It seemed as though several began to stop and talk to Dan and Denise as they passed by their home on evening walks. Dan had landscaped his yard beautifully, and many complimented him sincerely. Even before moving in, Dan had become friends with a neighbor across the street by the name of Brent. Brent was very kind and accepting. They became friends. A few months later, Brent was called to be Bishop of the new ward. He decided to personally home teach Dan and his family.

As Dan progressed, he and Denise decided the motorcycle was not practical at the time, and they sold it. This was difficult for him. One of the members of the ward, a banker by profession, noticed this. One day, he showed up at Dan's home on his semi-new Harley Davidson motorcycle and insisted that Dan take it for a ride. This impressed Dan, and another friendship began.

With time, Dan began to feel more comfortable in his association with members of the church. He even came to the neighborhood Halloween party. He made a great Captain Hook! He was visited by the Ward Mission leader, and agreed to meet the missionaries. When the missionaries arrived, however, he had changed his mind. It was difficult to make or keep spiritual commitments when there was little spiritual nourishment in his life. More time passed. As we prayed for an opportunity to share the gospel with Dan, an opportunity was provided.

Denise's eight-year-old daughter, from a previous marriage, reached the age of accountability and was preparing to be baptized. Knowing the kind of person Dan was, I knew he would be there. We invited the missionaries to attend the baptism and hopefully meet Dan. I knew that he would probably feel the spirit during the baptismal service, and that it would be a perfect time to invite him to listen to the discussions.

It was a beautiful service. Everyone present, including Dan, felt the Spirit. He was invited, and accepted the invitation. Later, when a companionship consisting of one full-time missionary and one stake missionary arrived at his home, he was not as eager to listen to their message. He did let them in, however, and two and a half hours later, they left. A wonderful experience had been had by all. The next day, that full-time missionary was transferred.

The stake missionary introduced Dan to the replacement, and the process continued. All of the discussions were taught with members present, sometimes several. Dan progressed cautiously. As the Elder's quorum heard about his investigating, they rallied also. When Dan expressed an interest in receiving help laying his sod, *eighteen* members of the quorum, several boys, two full-time missionaries and two stake missionaries showed up to help. The large yard was laid in less than an hour! Dan participated in a hay-hauling assignment at the welfare farm. He loved it.

After several weeks, Dan was baptized. Because I was present during the discussions, I can testify that He did not experience a social conversion only. He has a testimony of the truths of the restoration. He has tasted the sweetness of knowing that his sins, no matter how awful, can be forgiven. He continues to progress. We are good friends. It has not been easy for him. But then again, it is not easy for anyone.

He is not perfect. But the gospel has made a tremendous difference in his life. He has received the Priesthood and a church calling. As a home teacher he is ministering to the needs of others. And he is preparing to be sealed to Denise in the house of the Lord.

Who can tell the power of God? Who can comprehend the eternal significance of the missionary work each person did with Dan? It was no one person. It was the Lord, Dan, and the combined efforts of a neighborhood of saints that exposed him to the truths of the gospel in faith and invited the Spirit of the Lord to testify of their veracity. This is missionary work.

I will ever forget Dan. We will be life-long friends, and then some. None of those who were blessed to participate, as the hand of the Lord worked upon Dan, were perfect. No one performed any great and marvelous miracle. It was the Lord and Dan that did that. But the little acts of faith made a difference.

Missionary work is more than just fulfilling assignments. It has little to do with statistics. It has everything to do with faith in the Lord Jesus Christ. It has everything to do with helping our brothers and sisters here in mortality become more like Christ. As each of us partakes of His atonement, the Great Plan of Happiness has meaning in our lives.

Chapter 10 - The Work:
How Great Shall Be Your Joy

I. BLESSINGS OF THE WORK

The Lord blesses those who serve Him in many ways.

The Thing of Most Worth

Try to imagine what our Father in Heaven must feel as he watches the way many people live their lives. The many who suffer are *His children.* It is no wonder we are commanded so strongly to share. Indicative of His love for His children is the Lord's statement that, "the thing that will be of most worth" to those of us who have the truth, "will be to declare repentance" (D&C 15, 16). This truth is so important that two entire sections of the Doctrine and Covenants contain it alone (15,16).

There are many other blessings promised to those who will care enough to rescue our brothers and sisters in darkness. In James we are taught that , "he which converteth the sinner from the error of his way shall save a soul from death, and shall hide a multitude of sins" (5:20).

Modern church leaders have taught that not only are we helping to cover the sins of someone else by helping him or her repent and avoid further sin, but by sharing the gospel and serving righteously we can actually make partial restitution for our own previous sins.

Forgiveness of Our Sins

Speaking at Brigham Young Unversity, Elder Theodore M. Burton taught that service to others can help us progress spiritually and receive forgiveness of our sins.

"I am grateful for the Book of Mormon which explains how we can repay Jesus Christ for his great mercy to us. His sacrifice atoned even for our personal sins and makes his mercy available to you and to me.

"King Benjamin may have explained how repayment is possible in these words; `And behold, I tell you these things that ye may learn wisdom; that ye may learn that when ye are in the service of your fellow beings ye are only in the service of your God [Mosiah 2:17].' This service to others can include significant good works that could compensate Jesus for his restitution made for you.

"God's work and glory is to redeem his children. If we participate in this redemptive service, he pays us in blessings for which we qualify by that service. What this scripture then means is that you can repay Jesus for his mercy to you by being kind, thoughtful, considerate and helpful to those around you. By such service to others you can gradually pay back your indebtedness to your Savior. You can put the evil you have done out of your mind by charitable service to others.

"As you begin to repay your debt through service to your family, neighbors and friends, the painful elements of your sin will gradually fade from your mind. They will no longer fill your soul with anxiety and concern nor will you be plagued by worries over previous transgression. Instead of being filled with vain regrets over past deeds which are already done and which events you are powerless to change, you will now be so busy doing good works for others that you will not have a desire to sin or

THE WORK: HOW GREAT SHALL BE YOUR JOY

disobey, nor to recall past sin or disobedience"[16]

In the fall of 1831, the Lord told some of the early missionaries through the prophet Joseph that the missionary work they had been doing was so important to our Father and the angels in heaven that their "sins [were] forgiven [them]" (D&C 62:3).

In section 84, the Lord says, "For I will forgive you of your sins with this commandment--that you remain steadfast in your minds in solemnity and the spirit of prayer, in bearing testimony to all the world of those things which are communicated unto you" (vs. 61). These are rewards promised to anyone willing to put forth effort in sharing the gospel.

II. THE CONSEQUENCES OF LOVE

If you really want to make a difference, be a missionary.

Lives Changed

A good friend of mine is fond of saying that he knows the gospel is true because it changes lives. Throughout this book I have shared many true examples of successful missionary experiences. I have tried to share with you the outcomes of each of these examples of righteous missionary service to the best of my knowledge at the time of printing. It is easy to think of stories we read in books as simply stories. My witness to you is that the gospel does change real people's lives. It does so because learning and living according to its truths is a fundamental part of the purpose of mortality. And because of the nature of mortality, when one life changes, many others are affected as well.

---

[16]   From *The Meaning of Repentance*, BYU Fireside and Devotional Speeches, University Publications, 1984, p.99. Used by permission.

It may have seemed, at times, that these experiences were unusual or that one great thing changed a person's heart. I hastened to point out, that the road was long for almost everyone mentioned in this book. Conversion and change are almost never easy.

At the time of printing, the "Smith" family, who experienced all the opposition (Chapter Three), has experienced great change. Sister Smith has served faithfully in many callings, two of the three children have been on missions and Brother Smith has been called first as a counselor in the Bishopric and then as Bishop of the Ward where they live. Think of all the people that have now been blessed by their service to the Lord.

If the principles I have shared in this book have helped you, think of the effect Brother Art Paulson had by helping my father remain active in the church through the difficult teenage years. And the list goes on.

A Cause to Beat All Causes

When I was a teenager my father used to say to me, "Shane, when you die, the only things you get to take with you are your relationships with other people." He would then counsel me to be careful about how I treated people around me. He has always been good at dealing with people. Everybody likes Dad. I have come to realize that it is because Dad likes everybody. And I have noticed something else over the years. My Dad has always been happier than the average person. Love really does beget love.

In the 1960's the "hippie" movement was in full motion, and "finding yourself" was the big thing. Many a young person wasted some of the prime years of life exploring the paths of sin, only to discover that wickedness is not happiness. In fact, history is replete with examples of people trying to adopt the promotion of *something* of value as their life's quest. Everybody seems to want a cause to fight for--a standard to rally around.

Many a professional person, particularly at mid-life, has asked him or herself, "Does my life mean anything? Have I made a difference in the world? If I suddenly vanished, would there be any worthwhile legacy left behind?" Even people who have succeeded in amassing tremendous fortunes sometimes wonder if their introduction of the new "handy-dandy widget" has made any real lasting contribution to the good of society.

The Lord has provided a way for each of us to ensure that we will leave our mark on humanity--for eternity. May I be so bold as to suggest that the cause in which each of us can enlist is love. Everyone, regardless of occupation, race, nationality, etc., can share the restored gospel with others, thereby sharing the fullness of the love of God with humankind. The effects of that love will, in all reality, make significant, lasting differences and go a long way toward changing the world in real terms.

Changing the World

President Benson used to say, "The Lord works from the inside out. The world works from the outside in. The world would take people out of the slums. Christ takes the slums out of people, and then they take themselves out of the slums. The world would mold men by changing their environment. Christ changes men, who then change their environment. The world would shape human behavior, but Christ can change human nature.... Yes, Christ changes men, and changed men can change the world."[17]

I know a man of some reputation in his country. He was involved in politics and had even considered a run for the presidency because he was tired of what he felt was corruption in his government.

---

[17]   *Ensign,*, Conference Report, October, 1984. © The Church of Jesus Christ of Latter-day Saints. Used by permission.

He changed his mind, however, after he joined the church. As he experienced a mighty change of heart, he came to believe that it is not the laws of man that really govern people, but their hearts. He decided that as long as the people in the government were willing to be dishonest and corrupt, no amount of rule-changing or policing was going to solve the problem.

He resolved that the real solution to the problems of his country was to preach the gospel, for once the hearts of the people were changed, the people would no longer tolerate dishonesty and corruption. Every nation on earth could take a lesson from this man and benefit from this truth. Could there be a more noble cause than to change the world in this way?

A Chain is Broken

Not long ago, a friend shared with me and some of my associates at the MTC, a marvelous experience. He told about his conversion to the gospel. He did so by trying to help those of us present comprehend the chain of consequences and sin that had been going on in his family for generations. He came from an abusive home. Drugs, alcohol and immorality were also family traditions. For generations, these things had been going on.

After briefly recalling a few tragic incidents by way of illustration, he asked his wife to send his little son forward. A beautiful little three-year-old boy walked to the front of the room. He gently picked the boy up and held him tight. The child put his arms around his father's neck and hugged him. It was a beautiful scene.

This father then told how, because of his newfound knowledge of the truths of the restored gospel, his beautiful little son had not only never experienced any of the evils that he was subjected to as a child, but he also shared some of the opportunities his son was having that he never dreamed of having as a child. He then said simply, "The chain is broken."

Yet, a chain was also forged. Sharing the gospel with others is an opportunity to break chains of death and link families together with unbreakable chains of eternal lives. How could anyone possibly do anything more worthwhile? When we share the gospel with someone, we are doing something of eternal significance. We are enabling our brothers and sisters to become exalted.

These are the consequences of love. These are the inherent rewards of missionary work. To see the world changed, little by little, to know that we were blessed to participate in helping to establish the kingdom of God on earth, and to receive the blessings that come from fulfilling His commandment to share-- these are the effects of proclaiming His word.

Epilogue

As you begin to share the gospel, remember to help others stay focused on those things that will enable them to experience real, lasting conversion. Remember the conversion process (Chapter Five).

Questions

From time to time, those with whom you share will have questions. Most questions are honest attempts at discovering truth. But it is not the responsibility of any missionary to answer every question that is asked. Rather, it is to help others learn and apply *those truths that will enable them to experience true conversion.*

You may have heard the anecdote, "It does not necessarily matter whether the pearly gates swing open or slide open, *as long as they open.*" Try to avoid lengthy discussions of less-important principles. There are times when you should answer the questions that are *not* asked. Much time, effort and heartache can be avoided as you help others focus on the things that really matter.

This may be difficult. At times, the questions and concerns that are raised seem very important to the individual(s). Elder M. Russell Ballard tells of a friend who had developed some serious concerns about the truthfulness of the gospel and the church. He sought answers to specific questions about issues that, to him, seemed fundamental to his testimony.

EPILOGUE

The Spirit directed Elder Ballard, however, to guide the man, ever so tactfully, back to the Book of Mormon. The result was, that this man gained the spiritual foundation and insight that enabled him to understand things he never could have previously understood. The Spirit can teach in ways words never will.

What Really Matters

It is easy for those who are beginning to grasp the iron rod to be overcome by temptations and mists of darkness. Do not ignore the concerns of others, but remember that it is the Spirit that changes peoples minds and hearts. The Spirit testifies of truth. We help others experience spiritual conversion as we help them come in contact with the right truths. We need to teach them the messages of the restoration, by the Spirit, and do everything within our power to help them focus on gaining *spiritual* witnesses of these truths. Inviting people to read and pray about the Book of Mormon will be key in this process.

What You Know

When it comes to the things that really matter, chances are you already know the essentials. The gospel is beautifully simple. Do not allow yourself to be drawn into debates over things that are of little consequence (D&C 19:31). Bear your testimony. Share with others the witnesses you have received that God lives, that His Son Jesus Christ atoned for the sins of all mankind, that Joseph Smith was a prophet, that God has restored the true church of Jesus Christ to the earth, that God speaks through living prophets today, and that the Book of Mormon is true. Share specific ways in which these truths have blessed your life.

There is no room for debate with regard to what you *know*. As others question *how* you know, and you share with them appropriately, they will be opening the door to eternal life, and you will have brought them to the door and given them the key.

INDEX

131

INDEX

G

Gang, boy part of, 17
General Authorities, 29, 41, 76
God, relationship with, 12
Good, we seek all, 23
Gospel, of Jesus Christ, 31, the
    solution, 36
    how it is presented
    makes a difference, 89-
    90
Grandma and Grandpa, sharing
    bicycle experience, 1
Great things, 95, 107

H

Happiness, life quest for truth
    and, 28, sharing it, 1-3,
    great plan of, 2,
    wickedness not, 2,
    righteousness is, 2
Hinckley, Gordon B., 56
Home Teaching, 4, 97, 104-105
Hunter, Howard W., 36
Hunters and fishers of men, 98

I

Iron rod, helping grasp, 2

J

Jesus Christ, central figure in
    plan, 31, 106, will go
    before your face, 105
Joseph Smith, 5, 31, 65, 129
Joy, 2-3, Shall be great, 3, 121

K

Korea, experience in Seoul, 101

L

Leader of youth, 73
Learn and believe, 7
Lies, 9, adversary's common, 9
Light, 2-3, 9, of Christ, 14-16
Littlefield, Steven R., 74
Lives changed, 123
Love, of Eternal Father, 11,
    consequences of, 123,
    greater, 25, of a
    neighborhood,
    117, parental, 11, shown
    after doorstep rejection,
    60, teaches truth, 60-61,
    invites spirit, 62,
    prepares others for more
    truth, 62-63, 103

M

Making a difference, 86
Matters, what really, 129
Media, modern, 39
Message of the restoration, 31
Missionary, a prospective with
    weakness, 74 Don Pedro
    became, 113,
Missionary Work,
    defined, 2, 40, 57, 67,
    96-98, 99, 100, 120
    responsibility and
    opportunity, 1, 96
    summarized, 40,
    overcoming obstacles in,
    47, consequences of, 74
Monson, Thomas S., 8, 75

INDEX

INDEX